A 200th Anniversary Portrait

# DALHOUSIE UNIVERSITY

Poetry by GEORGE ELLIOTT CLARKE
Curated by MONA HOLMLUND

GOOSE LANE EDITIONS & DALHOUSIE UNIVERSITY

To Dalhousians past, present, and future.

Net proceeds from sales of this book support scholarships
for Indigenous and African Nova Scotian students.

Dalhousie University is grateful to our long-standing affinity partner,
TD Insurance Meloche Monnex,
for providing a copy of this 200th Anniversary book
to all graduates of 2018.

# CONTENTS

ELDERS' MESSAGE 5

PRESIDENT'S MESSAGE 7

"THE STORY OF DALHOUSIE;
OR, THE UNIVERSITY AS INSURGENCY"
by George Elliott Clarke 8

A PORTRAIT IN MEMORIES
by Mona Holmlund 23

1 BUILDINGS AND BOULEVARDS 27

2 A YEAR IN THE LIFE 51

3 QUEST FOR KNOWLEDGE 75

4 DAL IN THE WORLD 95

5 YOU WERE HERE 113

6 MY DAL 137

ACKNOWLEDGEMENTS
The Provenance of the Portrait 140

PHOTOGRAPHY CREDITS & ARCHIVAL CITATIONS 142

# ELDERS' MESSAGE

Nujikinamatnewoqom klwekutek Mikma'ki um'tki.

Dalhousie sits on unceded and unsurrendered land of the Mi'kmaq.

Elders-in-residence:
Elder Billy Lewis, Elder Deb Eisan, and Elder Geri Musqua-LeBlanc at the opening of Mawio'mi, 2017. (DA)

# PRESIDENT'S MESSAGE

In 1818, Lord Dalhousie, the colonial governor of Nova Scotia, proposed the establishment of a new college. Funded with the spoils of the War of 1812 and modelled on the University of Edinburgh, the new institution aspired to international standards and was to be open to all, regardless of class or religious belief. It was an ambitious vision, and one that caused the little college to struggle, particularly amidst sectarian loyalties in its early decades.

Two centuries later, Dalhousie University has grown from that little college by the sea to become a national and global leader, and the leading university in Atlantic Canada. Drawing on our founding values, we aspire to academic excellence, to have an impact on our local communities, and to become an inclusive institution where all truly belong.

Universities are deeply entwined in the lives of their community, and the history of Dalhousie has been made rich and varied by its people. Dal's history is shaped by esteemed students, faculty, staff, and alumni—poets, prime ministers, and a Nobel laureate—and by groundbreaking discovery across two centuries of engagement with community.

Dalhousie at its best has been driven by a threefold mission of teaching, research, and service, and by a commitment to values of excellence, intellectual rigour, freedom of inquiry and expression, and inclusion and respect for all persons. Like all institutions, we have both our successes and our very human frailties when measured against such high ideals. Yet, our story is one of continually renewed commitment to those ideals, taking our place among Canada's great universities to better serve our community and our world.

How to capture such a rich and complex story? This book takes two approaches: poetry and pictures. In his epic poem "The Story of Dalhousie; Or, The University as Insurgency," Dal alumnus and Canada's 7th Parliamentary Poet Laureate George Elliott Clarke lyrically captures Dalhousie's daunting history, illuminating who we have been and who we might become. The collections of images that follow form an impressionistic and evocative portrait of Dalhousie that emerges as a "family photo album" of our two centuries.

Dalhousie's 200th anniversary is an occasion to celebrate our past, thank those who have contributed to our success, and look to the future. Throughout these pages, see what we have achieved together, and dream about what's next.

Dr. Richard Florizone, Dalhousie's 11th President

# The Story of Dalhousie; Or, The University as Insurgency
GEORGE ELLIOTT CLARKE

I

Named for a Scottish castle at two streams where trout and salmon
flicker and gleam and splash,
and named for George Ramsay, whose prowess at Waterloo—
cannonading and negating Napoleon,
got him dubbed Lord,
"Dalhousie" originates as a trophy—a profit—of *War*,
as actual booty—
the twelve-thousand-Halifax-£ boodle
snatched from Brit-conquered Castine in Maine
and eyeballed in the Nova Scotia colony—
for paving stones, a garrison library, *et cetera*;
except that Lord Dalhousie—
now His Majesty's Lieutenant Governor of Nova Scotia
(due to his sorties and flourishes *contra* "Boney")—
noticed the New Scottish colony lacked a college
capable of sprouting its own Christian ministers
who'd spout—he prayed—open-door-fresh-air,
open-minded, *but* godly precepts—
inspired by the porridge, salmon, and whiskey of Edinburgh—
the Scottish Enlightenment, Rabbie Burns ecumenicalism
and Adam Smith firm-hand and clear-eye of Edinburgh—
and the brogue and Gaelic of grey-beige but bagpiped Edinburgh—
and the chill fog, dour granite, and indomitable thistle of Edinburgh—
and tolerate no spite, but be suave, urbane:
Was that the meaning of the corn, oil, and wine,
Lawd Dalhousie spilled on the cornerstone of his Haligonian university,
two years after the Prince Regent'd bleated "Oui," bureaucratically,
assenting to the eccentric notion of an ocean-side,
Scotian, non-sectarian college—
as of February 6, 1818?

George Elliott Clarke, Parliamentary Poet Laureate 2016–2017 and Dalhousie alumnus (MA 1989, LLD 1999), performing the 200th anniversary poem at the Bicentennial Launch, February 6, 2018, Rebecca Cohn Auditorium. (NP)

II

Just ten days after cannons' kabamming gunpowder
saluted resonantly the college's (university's) debut,
Lawd Dal'd slooped off to Ville de Québec,
to govern every Britannic inch of Amérique du Nord
(and latterly India),
if yet right oblivious to the politic primacy
of so-called East Indians, West Indians, and American Indians....
In any event, the founder exited,
and his Halifax namesake college—
rampant on the city's Grand Parade—
was just gonna have to duke it out—
go head-to-head, toe-to-toe, face-to-face—
with double-talking preachers and two-fisted priests—
all hotly redneck under their white collars—
agitated by a "non-denominational" school
that might siphon off sect-anointed moolah—
whether taxpayer or top-hatted, public or plutocratic—
so that Anglican, Baptist, Catholic, Methodist, and Presbyterian
township-and-county edifices of *Edification*,
would go begging for cash, begging for students,
begging for profs,
and end up bagging only draughty piles, half-scaffolding,
bleak in perspective and empty of prospects,
but resounding with ill winds blaring legislative *nyet, nyet, nyet*—
that nixing, niggardly *fiat*—
over foundation cracks bristling
theological nettles....
"Besides," fretted tonsured, whiskered ecclesiasts,
"Dalhousie ain't split off *ex* the Kirk:
It's a conspiracy of cloak-and-dagger Presbyterians!"

III

King's College spurned entanglement with Dal;
born skeptical, infant Acadia—askance—glanced at Dal;
newborn St. Mary's could only eye Dal as suspect:
"One united College for Nova Scotia was dangerous
[*circa* 1843],
for how could clergy doctrinally discriminate
a Catholic microscope from a Baptist telescope,
a Methodist microbe from an Anglican asteroid?"
Surely, colleges conniving to be classed as universities
needed congregations for *Conscience* and cash flow!
Joe Howe fulminated *Reaction*: "Nova Scotia's plagued
by black-hatted, black-coated, black-horse-riding,
black-Bible-brandishing blackguards—
a retrograde, degenerate, backward *avant-garde*—
pinch-faced, presbyopic profs—
who can debate Satan in Latin,
and who wager New Glasgow
and New Minas
all suitable for resuscitated, old-stock *Feudalism*:
'Better to be rebarbative, provincial,' they allege,
'than rambunctious, experimental, secular,
or else Halifax annexes Hell.'"

IV

By 1847, Dalhousie was classless, penniless, friendless,
studentless, professorless, and so less and less a college,
it did seem, said some, well-nigh worthless....
Except, it could be a High School—
*circa* 1856—

and languish in such *louche*, secondary status,
serving up fish-'n'-chips rather than physics . . . .
Unless the Presbyterians could comport and sport
as the Trojan Horses of *Liberal Education*
*vis-à-vis* the ABCs—
Anglicans/Baptists/Catholics—
and the mathematical (atom-and-hair-splitting),
anti-human-anatomical Methodists—
by letting Dalhousie docs teach Everyman,
while church-connected campuses corral their clergy
on keeps agog at Haligonian grog shops—
on redoubts spurning petticoats and rum—
the temptations of molasses
and Mephistophelian tobacco,
where *Virtue* is apprehended by declining always
that Euro-trash, exploitative spectacle—the Waltz . . . .

    v

1863 marks the reset, the resurrection,
when what was Dalhousie College
is once more Dalhousie College,
but now cheek-by-jowl with a brewery—
proffering ale for every ailment—
and profs on tap
to discourse on trout fishing at Salmon River (Dartmouth)
or to wield Euclidean equations like sledgehammers
(that best beer bottles at bustin' open a skull).
The Dal rhetoricians be eristic and exigent chaps,
step-dancing among "Crimean heroes"
dead-drunk in downtown gutters or in backyard mud,

while their couple-dozen students fortify their bellies
(from which all soliloquies surface)
with oatmeal gruel, salt cod, corned beef, bread, apples,
molasses, potatoes—
a "quantum of solace"—of rum . . . .

    vi

*Science* evolves outta sickness and the Genesis damnation,
declaring *Birth* ushers *Sin*-struck mortals
soon-or-late to an earthen berth—
a point as true for Dal Natural Philosophers
lisping the 1870 motto,
"*Ora et labora*"
("Pray and work")
as it be for any lad (and lady).
So, despite the Anatomy Act gravely allowing docs
to carve up any indigent (poorhouse) cadaver,
there befell a shortage of corpses
to analyze—cannibalize—
so as to advance, *convincingly*,
life-saving *Medicine*.
The fix demands a Medical Faculty—
a separate body bestowing Dal degrees—
in spluttering fits and seizure starts—
in the 1870s,
until, by degrees,
the Halifax School of Medicine becomes separate—
but mediocre—
by 1885,
shrouding the parturiating in prudish, Victorian cloaks,

applying Jack-the-Ripper willy-nilly to callously plucky cadavers,
that is, until Greco-Latinate Flexner came calling
to castigate the med-school as "grossly appalling,"
thus triggering its upbraiding "upgrade"—absorption—by Dal,
*circa* 1911,
and later, nigh 1920,
access to a tramline, Public Health Clinic
(where students could describe and doctors prescribe),
sponsored by Mr. Rockefeller and Mr. Carnegie—
pleased to prop up latter-day—if rustic—
salt-spray, hayseed Scots.

VII

*Pace* the messy stillbirth of the University of Halifax
(deceased 1881)—
that effort to mollify church-campus envy of Dal
and to unify Babel-Pentecostal, Christian syllabi
(conflicting dogmas barked in passionate tongues)—
by asking a single Congress of Examiners to test
would-be clerics and should-be clerks;
anent that good-intentioned, but goddamned gaffe;
Dalhousie was set to vaunt—flaunt—itself—
but only if private coin could coddle its Liberalism,
preserving it from whimsical chastisement
by skinflint and/or shrewish public finance.
Thus commences the dedicated schmoozing of donors,
benefactors, citizens who'll morph from Midas to Apollo—
those enlightened, eleemosynary few
whose munificence is gold showering down like sunlight.
Soon, George Munro professorships, George Munro bursaries,

free Dal to headhunt scholars and bodysnatch students,
to internationalize the regional reach,
to pick off Cambridge, Edinburgh, Harvard, Oxford alumni-luminaries
and transplant 'em as elect, *Acadiensis* profs,
sure to entrance—intrigue—undergrads....
Here's how the bar-and-brothel-adjacent college—
(1880s)—
commences a romance with worldly, surplus *Capital*,
to wine and dine well-endowed, well-read widows
and moneybags pining to be labelled "Dr."
(but skipping the bothersome dissertation);
and whose deliberated, fiscal *Realism*
(not really *Cynicism*),
means the college can afford to front as airily sophisticated—
float a cosmopolitan, espresso-and-Spinoza aura—
chic as Harvard Square, Broadway, Piccadilly, Old Town, the Quartier Latin,
if never so posh (quite)....

VIII

The other mind-expanding, mood-altering revolution—
besides the fluxing influx
of boffo, ego-stroking, self-aggrandizing,
adventurist donations—
is the entrance of women, politic *arrivistes* opposing
(unmanly, inhumanly practiced) man-only *Empowerment*....
Register here that Dal never opposed
registering women,
though the upstart distaff only alighted in the 1880s—
idealistic church ministers' daughters
(or lasses consigned purses by deceased papas)—

spurred on by Munro's gilded disbursements,
and not keen on expected subservience to hubbies,
but pooh-poohing patriarchal folderol
(that mantra that "Male Rule" is an Adamic mandate),
and preferring Economics to that desperately poor sister—
"Home Ec"—
and meditating on Madame Curie rather than mastering cookery.
'Tis necessary to place women up front in the classroom:
Let fellas stand when the ladies enter;
remain seated as the feminists exit.

    IX

Ask not about "Coloured" pupils!
Local ex-slaves—
and/or descendants of Loyalists, Maroons, Refugees, Fugitives—
attaining Grade Three—
maybe—miraculously—Grade Six—
in Negro-only, one-room shacks—
have a difficult-to-impossible time
to sidle into Dal (*de facto*, white, aristocratic) classes.
Yet, a few West Indians and Bermudans can/do.
Check Sylvester Williams, ex-Trinidad/Tobago,
who took up Dal Law by 1893,
and departed minus the degree,
but still rallied the Pan-African Movement
to espouse—Empire-wide—
African and Black and Caribbean independence,
that is, escape from European/Caucasian "uplift"
(or *Downpression*)....

But let us not forget Halifax's James R. Johnston,
who became Dal's first Black Bachelor of Letters—1896,
next a Law grad—1898,
and whose moniker now graces Dal's Chair in Black Studies.
(And mark the residency of Africadian contralto,
Portia White, at Shirreff Hall, *circa* 1929.)

    X

1887: Dal transits off the Grand Parade—
takes to heights above Halifax's Northwest Arm—
and shows aspects tricked out in brick, not stone;
that same year, *Law* materializes—concretizes—
with a Constitutional-Law-magisterial dean
who's a Member of Parliament—
and a decade later,
with a Contracts prof who's—ditto—
a Member of Parliament—
while Engineering barged into the calendar—
thanks to coal mining for engines, steamships, furnaces;
next, all the emitted soot and grit and dirt and cinders
encouraged Civil Engineering—
roads, bridges, tunnels—
the cornerstones and buttresses of *Industry*,
but also the Marxmen's *forte*.
(Yet, conscription *Communism* entails *Construction*
as shoddy as *Capitalism*'s manufactured ephemera....
Seldom does the cement set strong and smooth;
rather, it cracks:
Compare the Great Wall of China and the Berlin Wall.)

XI

1911-12, *antebellum*,
the Dal Forward Movement figures to finagle $300,000
to field triple schematics—
a library, *Science* laboratories,
and, at Studley, space for *Medicine* and *Dentistry*,
featuring Georgian conjurations of local ironstone,
plus quarters to round up students and round em off....
Shouldn't undergrads canoodle in their own courtly alcoves?
Thus, circulated blueprints on June 29, 1914,
the day after Archduke Ferdinand and his missus
became the bull's eyes for bullets booming, *"War!"*

XII

Is a scholar as manly as a soldier?
Decidedly positive were the Dal recruits
who lined up for Lord Kitchener,
though—soon—Krupp guns chopped down scores....
Assuredly, Krauts were keener in their aim
than were Brit generals in their tactics,
stupidly self-assured that The Great War
was just a blow-up of Waterloo,
that guys affixing bayonets—
could charge suddenly, frontally, frantically at machine guns—
or get splattered by shells
and/or scattered by caustic, lacerating, and/or choking gas—
and still stand triumphant, rosy cheeked, laurelled,
to warble "Cheerio" to the Kaiser.

No matter: The Albion Canucks—
sporting maple-leaf badges on khaki lapels—
enlisted holus-bolus the Dalhousie men,
so that females numbered 2/3 of *Arts* classes,
and then the Canadian Corps were "over the top"
on the Western Front,
hammering dead the *Götterdämmerung* "Huns" so damn much,
the "Jerries" slammed 'em as "Shock Troops."

XIII

While the Great War waxed, waned, Dal erected
the MacDonald Memorial Library
which inaugurated—for the entire Dominion—
the Library of Congress cataloguing system;
while the Law School now accented lucrative practicalities—
not supposed eccentricities like the Constitution
or various forms of execution.
(What's the ideal form of State murder?
The noose, the guillotine, or the electric chair?
Would you rather snap your neck, lose your head, or fry?)
Still, despite its distance, the *War* wracked Dal:
The double-vessel collision in Halifax Harbour—
December 6, 1917—
discharged battering and bashing power equivalent
to three thousand kilotons of TNT detonating instantly—
and North End Halifax got obliterated,
vanishing under an unprecedented,
dented-bent-stovepipe-shaped, fuming cloud
(an augury of A-bomb and H-bomb

Doomsday *Meteorology*)—
and a blast that turned windows into daggers
and metal into a shower of molten slag.
The gargoyle-faced, monstrously punctured survivors
of the two thousand slain pretty much outright,
got bandaged angelically by Dal med apprentices
and by Jane Austen essayists instantly deputized as nurses;
and the Carnegie Foundation okayed snappily
bankrolling the dispatch of glaziers and masons
to patch Dal's fractures—plus those windows now wounds.

XIV

*Postbellum*, Jennie Shirreff Eddy found herself wooed
by Dal grad and future Prime Minister of Canada
(Rt. Hon.) R.B. Bennett
to pay out a tad of her matchstick-
and-toilet-paper-fortune
(racked up by E.B. Eddy)
to deck out a women's residence—
Shirreff Hall—
in pink quartzite ex-New Minas.
Next the men's residence—
Pine Hill—
got promulgated in 1919,
thanks to the purchase of a Northwest Arm hotel
for $160,000
outta the Million Dollar (cash-scoop-up) Campaign.

XV

Flames dissecting King's College in 1920 resurrected
the spectre of *Amalgamation*,
not just of Dal and King's,
but of all the church-linked Atlantic colleges—
if all could be egged on to accept $3 million
in Carnegie Foundation "bread" (i.e., *Bribery*).
By the finish of the 1920s, the federation idea
was finished,
its very inception seemingly meretricious,
and the Carnegie bucks flocked back
to plump up in stony banks and nest in lambskin briefcases,
and Dal was left to worry
whether it would decline into an ivied, vocational school,
graduating lawyers as practical as carpenters;
doctors less dexterous—
but more lethally arrogant—
than butchers;
engineers talented at concocting white elephants;
and Humanities students
whose Latin announced *casus belli*
and/or pronounced *caveat emptor*.
Was it feasible for twentieth-century,
North American, industrial/commercial society—
so cavalierly results oriented
(always dreaming up a better machine gun)—
to value a brine-washed Canuck brain trust
capitalizing on buttoned-down scholars?

## XVI

Modernity whelps talkies and speakeasies,
Prohibition (of alcohol) and Revolution (by Lenin's Reds,
chased by Mussolini's Black Shirts),
*The Waste Land* in poetry
and *The Great Dictator* in film,
Duke Ellington veering Dixieland to bebop
and the Gershwin Bros. working Dixieland into Debussy....
Unable to stomach the hunger of Soviet Five-Year Plans,
and refusing to eat the lead of Fascist *coup* and Nazi *Putsch*,
suddenly cometh the (White) Russians—
landing right after Trotsky the Wobbly
(latterly toppled by a Mexican ice pick)
was sprung from his cell in Halifax's Citadel
to vamoose to St. Petersburg
to bully on the Bolshevik *bouleversement* of the *boulevardier* Czar;
Fleeing now also were Europe's Jews—
antennaed witnesses of Gulag
and prophets of Darwinian Death Camps—
voyaging to Pier 21 (Halifax),
finding entrée at Dalhousie (finally)—
reinforcing the possibility of string quartets serenading
otherwise jitterbugging sailors and their lindy-hopping molls,
and stressing Old World *savoir faire*, savvy,
in a city quite comfy with grungy *Vice*,
where *Adult Education* got started
primarily as a way to tamp down
the wartime spike in Venereal Disease....

## XVII

World War I gone, but World War II not yet,
Dal enrolments doubled—tripled—in between,
and then profound, radio orator—Herbert Leslie Stewart—
dreamt up—drafted—*The Dalhousie Review*,
a "Little Magazine" to rival McGill's *Fortnightly Review*
and maybe Chicago's *Poetry*,
which readers could sink their teeth into
while experiencing—with prayer and dread—
the operative know-how of the newfangled School of Dentistry.
Suddenly, Dal students staff a union
and Dal's president wins a house (of his own),
and the Dal coeds need shortened skirts
to suit Jazz Age, upsy-daisy, dipsy-doodle cavorting,
regardless of the acidic chagrin—
tut-tutting male killjoys, spoilsports,
dudes (duds), Dudley-do-wrongs exude—
those who should beg a Billy Butler Yeats–style
monkey-gland surgery—
that precursor to sildenafil citrate....

## XVIII

Sayeth Wall Street and bayeth Bay Street,
and screecheth the City and the Bourse (until hoarse):
"Sire no more MAs, but only MBAs:
We want '*Relevance*,' not '*Elevation*'!"
They're right? Or just brain-dead rightists?
Yet, how does acquaintance with Aristotle
elucidate investment portfolio profitability, *really*,

and how does memorization of Milton
aid the race to be the first to weaponize atoms—
the very guts of sunlight,
to incinerate a hundred thousand infants
in a thousandth of a second?
Eventually, Dal's George P. Grant, *philosophe*,
is gonna scorn the utility of the "multiversity,"
accusing it of most foul *Vainglory*,
in defining *Progress* as shifting from enumerating angels
prancing on a pinhead
to counting up the number of rat droppings one encounters
in a typical polio-, TB-, VD-ridden slum.
That's the age-old problem of this New Age:
When is knowledge *Wisdom*?
If ever, even?

    xix

Plots—policies—quicken when Angus L. invades the NS
Legislative Assembly, 1935,
unassailable at *Reform*, the local F.D.R.
(Fiercely Devoted Renovator)
votes in a refurbished Dalhousie Act,
though if he had his druthers,
he'd design one universal, Maritime university
rather than deign to tolerate
thirteen old-dog, old-boy, persnickety, church-college bastions
"worse than high schools"....
Then, out of Europe's swirling, Machiavellian-malevolent maelstrom,
whirls into town Lothar Richter, a fugitive intelligence,
to plant Dal's Institute of Public Affairs

and its eponymous, academic organ,
after first introducing himself ("*Guten Tag*") as a lecturer in German.
Currently, Dal's Chairman of the Board's a suave, Frank Sinatra type,
liking menthol cigarettes—three packs daily—
liking Scotch—three pungent tumblers daily,
while mover-and-shaker Prez'dent Stanley spoils to spiff up
Dal's Medical *et* Dental schools,
but *Depression*-depressed governors retort—
"The blind and deaf—poor and helpless—need aid, yep,
but not medico-dento apprentices,
bound to join the gold-plated, silver-spoon upper-crust...."

    xx

1939 detonates World-Wide War *redux*—
as Darwin's devils haste to gobble up territories
and gut, gas, and torch—"scientifically"—millions,
asserting mere "vermin extermination"—
thereby expanding to Europe and Asia.
past imperial European—imperious—*Evil*
in Africa, the Americas, and Asia,
but now all mechanical—as well as mechanized—
industrialized, efficient, mass-produced massacres.
Makes sense to open, in 1941,
Dal's Department of Psychiatry—
a testament to *Reason*, *Rationality*, *Mindfulness*—
even though the septic bias
of war-dirtied Halifax's white-coated, downtown doctors
prevents three Austrian refugee Jews
(escapees from Hitler's Semitic-genocidal regime)
from being able to Canadianize their med training

(August 1942) at Dal....
Too, while white students, white profs, and white troops
had green lights—*carte blanche*—to enjoy the Green Lantern's fare,
Coloured People (Negroes) had to forego taking meals there.
They could aim guns at Hitlerian *White Supremacy*,
but they couldn't stick a fork in it in the Halifax eatery.
Might as well ride the ferry footing Oakland Road
'cross the Northwest Arm to the Dingle,
then back again, price just 10¢,
while debating Poli Sci with Prez Stanley—
who deplored Dal's existence as a jewel
begrimed by a city slimy with slums....

    xxi

Mussolini got bulleted, then strung up by the heels;
Hitler gnawed a gat and then blazed to char;
Tojo dangled his avoirdupois from a strangling noose;
"hard and bitter" was the on-again *Peace*—
*Pax Americana* nipping at the Iron Curtain—
as Winnie (Pooh-Bah, Pooh-Bear) Churchill opined....
Thus, now Canuck vets gangwayed into Dal—
gleeful to exchange uniforms and sun-dazzling boots
for jackets, ties, and sun-dazzling shoes—
and deem textbooks now as precious as ale—
if not as alluring as the silk-stocking'd "sweater girls,"
still segregated sweetly in classroom front rows,
giving gents their backs,
their ponytails and bouncing curls;
so that forthright fellas had to face fantasies
by ogling *Esquire*'s nylon'd pin-ups.

The student army milling and marching,
taking one subject by storm
then overtaking others,
wresting and wrestling degrees from Dal,
necessitated instituting a Department of Graduate Studies,
as of 1948-49,
when bombastic Soviets set off an A-bomb at last—
and Mao unfurled a gold-star-spangled Red Flag over China—
and mandatory Latin sang its swan song,
croaking out in Oktoberfest beer fiestas at the Lord Nelson Tavern....
(Hear ye, hear ye:
Lusty, Bluenose, Ecum Secum yinkyank drowned out, *ipso facto*,
the fusty and musty, gusty and dusty,
dictation of literally guttural—and/or lyrical—grammarians....)

    xxii

Recognizing that Dal Law was in a parlous state,
due to formerly stingy, belly-tightening finance,
Premier Macdonald remedied the starvation,
tossing scrawny lawyers chunks of red meat
from the provincial budget (sausage-making) table.
Dentistry's decaying facilities also needed straightening—
and the filling in of architectural cavities with gold.
However, half the Atlantic governments,
all four of which ought to've backed the mouthy school,
gave *nada*, precisely zilch, just hot air,
leaving NS and NB to inject 25% of the filling
and/or pain-relief,
so Dalhousie had to repair the maw
3/4 solo,

digesting the corrosive, capital debt.
Meanwhile, the Medical Faculty were jaundiced—
distempered to—reflex—revolt—
no matter expertise in jigsawing through cadavers
or in rigging the jigging of an "Eye-Opener"
(gin, lemon, and Eno's Fruit Salts),
due to the irksome "busybody," Prez Kerr—
intruding picayune pencil counting,
while yielding insultingly insufficient funds
to let anyone win at research-grant roulette.
Well, everywhere, *Deterioration* is cured
by spreading the guilt around,
to petition plutocrats to forego gilt and give gold....
Enter Sir James Dunn and his widow, Lady Dunn,
whose largesse cranes up a new *Science* building—
despite blandishments and overtures and marriage proposal
(accepted) from U. New Brunswick's Lord Beaverbrook
(once upon a time sympathetic, appeasingly, to Hitler)—
and despite the dullard and dulling rejection
of celebratory liquor by Dal's teetotally sobre Prez Kerr—
Dunn's millions soon mint law scholarships;
and later bequeath Sir James's name to marquee a theatre;
all this construction adding to the not-incorrect perception
that Dalhousie was the most dynamic concentration
of intellects—
and intellectuals
(there's a distinction)—
on the Nor'East North Atlantic—
even if Beaverbrook hooded glamour-puss J.F.K. himself,
the latter granted a UNB-brand LLD
(1957).

XXIII

Just as J.F.K.'s New Frontiersmen
sent Ike and Tricky Dick packing,
so did testy profs like Geo Grant—
or Futurist librarian-poets like Doug Lochhead—
and others doubtful about Prez Kerr's prudence—
(if not prudery)—
get packing,
trekking down the road to Hogtown,
to address "New Lectures to a New Generation,"
now that the '60s were twisting and Hula Hooping in,
with Capitalist napalm for "Commies"—
colour TV for "consumers"—
cops' batons for the noggins of Civil Rights protestors
(daring to dream of eating, living, learning, sleeping,
wherever they could afford,
without regard to colour, creed, or committed *Faith*)....
And never ought a prude object
to comic pleasures, bawdy laughter,
lest his/her constituency disintegrate,
doubled up, howling;
yet, such a *dégringolade* degraded Kerr's standing—
so he was no longer pivotal,
but teetering,
and—ergo—unwelcome
(as of 1957).

XXIV

The 1960s summoned forth innovative policies,
*avant-garde* ideas,
but brandished inventive calamities
arising from old bigotries.
Thus, just two years after Prof. Guy Henson documented
*The Condition of the Negroes of Halifax City* (1962),
the sesquicentennial-old hamlet of Africville
began to be bulldozed into rubble,
a devastation imped by Dal *Social Work* theory,
Dal *Urban Planning* models,
although Dal scholars also totted up the faults
and tabulated the grim incivility
of "The Africville Relocation"
(that euphemism for South African *apartheid*–style
"Township Clearance")….
While Africville was being reclaimed by city planners
and civil engineers
(and rampaging rats and squabbling seagulls),
Dorothy Killam returned to Dal—
a widow also with a memory to further,
and whose treasure chest would nurture a library
and a children's hospital
(the latter separate from Dal)—
plus-plus-plus,
essentially thirty million bucks—
Dal's biggest bequest ever—
to magnet meritorious scientists,
buck up the Graduate School,
lavish scholarships whose gilt edges
could attract incandescent, foreign students.
Moreover, once New Brunswick aye-ayed funding
the nursing of New Brunswick interns
greenhoused in Dal's Medical School,
now feasible was the Sir Charles Tupper Medical Building.
Concurrently cemented was the Weldon Law Building,
and Lady Dunn re-emerged as Lady Beaverbrook
(doubly widowed now),
to christen the Sir James Dunn Law Library,
prefacing '67's "Summer of Love."
And Dal learners put up their own Student Union Building:
Finally, Rebecca Cohn's estate issues Dal $400,000
to complement all the newfangled, professional ziggurats
with a reminder of the spiritually minded *Arts*—
an auditorium sounding her name….

XXV

Apart from the spree—the spate—
breaking ground at breakneck speed—
of Dal structures of concrete and glass—
disdainful of old-school architecture—
students also are impatient with old structures,
for LSD
(*Liberty! Sex! Drugs!*)
seem(s) to highlight the *Hypocrisy—Illegitimacy—*
of the chilling, blood-curdling, Cold War propositions,
such as "Mutual Assured Destruction" in a thermonuclear exchange
is permissible,

and preferable to compromise—*détente*—with "Commies,"
and is defensible,
but not profanity and graffiti
(both corrosive of civil society),
and neither short skirts nor long hair.
Rightly, leftists forthrightly ridiculed such idiocy.
Yet, the sophomoric occupation of Prez Hicks's office
in September 1970—
a month before the dead-aim *Terrorism*
of Québécois kidnappers and assassins—
was only a namby-pamby, playacting gesture,
'cos everybody vacated the quarters
before cops could gun-point squatters out
and before Dal's Hicks returned from a non-eventful trip
to an uneventful non-event....
Arguably, anyway, the most rad uptakes at Dal
were the Transition Year Program
and the later Indigenous Black and Mi'kmaq Law Initiative,
both urged on by Burnley "Rocky" Jones's analysis—
to wit, that one way that the poor and Indigenous,
the criminalized and "Coloured,"
remain perpetual paupers, social outsiders,
is *via* their supposed inadmissibility to university
and law-school palaver—
those organs and engines of bourgeois hegemony.
Add to these programs the Maritime School of Social Work
and Dal Legal Aid,
and Dal evolves into a nexus, a matrix,
of potential change agents (i.e., Saul Alinsky acolytes)....
Thus, Halifax social worker Alexa McDonough,

straight outta Dal,
emerges to helm the New Democratic Party in NS
and then head the federal NDP—
those sock-and-sandal, tie-dyed and tea-tippling socialists,
"Only in Canada, eh? Pity!"

    XXVI

Dalhousie University's history is now two hundred years—and counting,
existing before me (and you),
and likely persisting eternally after us.
I dread to intersect my mortal bio with what is—
in comparison—deathless,
but I'm twice a Dal alumnus
(MA—1989; LLD—1999),
and long before either passage,
I was a Black Haligonian—
an Africadian—
inspired by an institution that is,
that excellent devise—a schooled insurgency—
summoning, perennially, "Young Turks"
to "Make It New" (*pace* Chu Tsi)—
make everything new—
by turning sailors into seismologists,
fishers into philosophers.
The Dalhousie difference was in making
all Halifax an extension campus—
a *de facto* university of the Commons
and the Public Gardens
and the waterfront-harboured, Palladian legislature,

even metaphysically unkillable Africville....
Thus, as a boy, my teeth got filled and fixed
and drilled and extracted
at the Dal clinic;
At 15, to design a Grade-9-junior-high-school A-bomb,
I biked down to the Killam Library,
and wantonly photocopied so many volumes,
I was practically kayoed by the acrid, ammonia fumes;
aged 17-19, I fellow-travelled with Rocky Jones's
TYP crew, debating "Black Liberation":
*Was it possible? In Nova Scotia?*
(Well, turntable Malcolm's agit-prop; turn up for talks on Mao.)
At age 21, visiting the Killam at Christmas,
trying to anatomize "Rabbi(e)" Dylan's "Like a Rolling Stone,"
I was so engrossed in my amateur Musicology
that I was padlocked therein the library.
Then, age 26, I arrived elect at Dal, selecting,
preternaturally, *the* John Fraser's
"Tradition and Experimentation in Modern Poetry,
1880-1920,"
a graduated (in terms of increasing insight) grad course,
that the *Calendar* certified as "ideal for poets."
Nicely, Doc Fraser (ex-Cambridge U.)
was easygoing, but no nice-and-easy prof.
His three-hour, Monday-night, living room–staged class
was an arena amid a library amid an art gallery,
with a tabby cat prowling round the coffee
or tea cups
and the cookie tray—
before the vivid, florid oils of Carol Hoorn Fraser—

and ten wise guys and bluestockings
tussling over Gothicism in Baudelaire,
surrealism in Hopkins,
Uncle Tom Eliot's Ol' Possum affecting of gloom-infected Laforgue,
and imagism conjuring sadism in *Hugh Selwyn Mauberley*.
Sure: I was a poet before I ambled into Fraser's chivalric ring
of knightly, smart-aleck, gladiatorial combat;
but I knew I'd earned the sobriquet, the designation, the lordship,
if one likes—
by fighting off the naysayers.

And this anecdote showcases, I pray,
Dalhousie's daunting history:
Hauntingly dauntless.

# A PORTRAIT IN MEMORIES
by Mona Holmlund

No one person has seen all of Dalhousie: all its iterations, all the personalities that helped to form it and have, in turn, been formed by it. This book is a witness to the University's two hundred years. It is a cloud chamber, a place where transformation in time and space has been frozen, offering glimpses into multiple memories. Some depict times that no one now living can personally summon; others capture what feels like today. Such a kaleidoscopic perspective lets us see across time, invites us to reflect—even meditate—on these objects, images, and moments to consider what they could have meant to someone else. The meaning of the University though, like the campuses themselves, expands and evolves. On these pages you will see Dal's growth from a single building on the Grand Parade in Halifax to five widely spread out campuses, from Saint John, New Brunswick, to Truro, Nova Scotia.

Our memories are made of fragmented images. We have become accustomed to understanding "history"—the stories we tell ourselves about ourselves—through pictures. We select, preserve, and communicate our sense of self through a kind of portraiture. Museums and galleries, films and documentaries, even news and selfies all reflect our longing for our history—our selves—to be reflected, to be seen, and to be known.

This curated collection of images spans Dal's history, offering glimpses of the memories of other Dalhousians and our relationship with one another. The juxtapositions may feel evocative and nostalgic or surprising and challenging. For some, their Dal no longer physically exists in the paths and buildings, in the people who laughed and learned together, the objects held, the clothes worn. Your experience of Dalhousie is not like anyone else's. Dalhousie is continually in flux, not just over two hundred years, but moment by moment, as individual lives move through it.

George Elliott Clarke's epic poem gives us one story of Dalhousie. He has painted a portrait of the ebb and flow, the push and pull (without pulling any punches) of the behemoth University's yearning, stumbling, toward progress. Clarke's poem is framed, finally, through the lens of his own life and his own time at Dal. The pictures here pick up where the poetry leaves off, in moments and memories from innumerable experiences of Dalhousie.

(DA)

There is not one singular, totalizing story to be told, but rather an impressionistic portrait composed of a multitude of memories, drawing on various "histories" of Dal. There are images here from P.B. Waite's *The Lives of Dalhousie*, from Brian Smith's *A Time to Remember*, and from editions old and new of the *Alumni News*, the *Dalhousie Gazette*, *DAL Magazine*, and *Dal News*. It commemorates our 200th anniversary celebrations with stills from websites and videos. There are also images and objects that haven't been seen before, unearthed from the Dalhousie University Archives, alongside custom photographs taken just for this collection.

Ultimately, this book is a family photo album. Its gaps and discontinuities, its diverse relationships and experiences are bound together by our shared attachment to this place. In these images we move through the spaces and seasons, the searching and service, the students and staff that, collectively, constitute the University. This book is an invitation to reminisce and preserve your own place in the unfolding story of Dalhousie.

That story is ultimately hopeful. George Elliott Clarke's poem suggests that the university can be a place of uprising. In another hundred years, we, and much of what we see around us, will be supplanted. Our landscapes will change. New symbols will replace well-worn objects. For now, while we look back on what Dalhousie has meant to us, we can also imagine what it could become. Dal's third century is the beginning of that next chapter. Between the poetry and the pictures is the space of possibility. In this illustration of our past and present we can imagine a future portrait created by new Dalhousians. Just picture it.

# BUILDINGS AND BOULEVARDS

"The best looking Campus in Canada."
— John Hugh MacLennan (Class of 1928),
*Dalhousie Alumni Magazine*, Winter 1989

Universities are much more than bricks and mortar. Yet, Dalhousie's physical presence has made an indelible impression on all who have been part of the University. The first association we have with an institution, especially one as complex and potentially abstract as a university, is through its landscape: its buildings and grounds, its pathways and vistas. To be "on campus" comes to evoke a sense of belonging and returning. Distinctive juxtapositions define the campus collage: historic stone and brick, modern glass and steel, enveloped by their urban settings. All of this against the backdrop of the sea, with the coastline, glimpsed or imagined, around every corner.

The memories assembled in this chapter interpret the ways the Dal campuses — Studley, Carleton, Sexton in Halifax, Agriculture at Truro, and Dalhousie Medicine New Brunswick in Saint John — have changed over time. Architecture matters. Dal's ironstone walls recall our traditions. The ivy-covered buildings embody our aspirations. The new structures articulate our ambitions. Public spaces create public cultures. We become part of them, and they, in turn, become part of us, reflecting our sense of place and our attachments. Dalhousie is continuously recreated — other Dalhousians have moved through different buildings and very different landscapes — as we each inscribe our own stories onto the mutable canvas of the campus.

opposite: Mi'kmaq Grand Keptin Antle Denny and President Richard Florizone install the Mi'kmaq flag on the Studley Quad, together, hand over hand, October 2016. (DA)

right: Atlantic Canada as depicted in 1625. (UA)

"Indigenous peoples, including the Mi'kmaq of Nova Scotia, have fought to preserve traditions and culture… This strength is now being displayed, through the flag, as a visible symbol on campus.… The Mi'kmaq did not cede the land of Mi'kma'ki to the Crown. The treaties were signed between the Mi'kmaq and the Crown to celebrate peace and friendship. In this spirit… as well as reconciliation, it is important for non-Indigenous community members to learn more about Mi'kmaq culture and become educated on Indigenous issues."

— Valerie Armstrong, Paqtnkek Mi'kmaw Nation, (BA 2016), Administrative Assistant, Indigenous Blacks and Mi'kmaq Initiative

(DU)

"His Royal Highness has been pleased to express his entire approbation of the funds in question being applied in the foundation of a Seminary in Halifax, for the higher Classes of Learning, and toward the Establishment of a Garrison Library."

— Governor General George Ramsay, the ninth Earl of Dalhousie, received approval for a proposed university in Halifax, February 6, 1818.

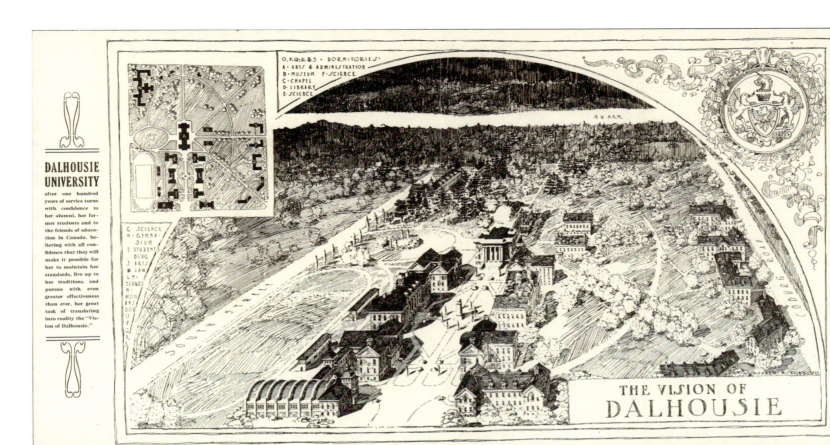

> "It is a city of strange sights, especially so to an eye bred inland. The most engaging of these owe their charm to the presence of the sea. At every turn, you are reminded of the ocean and the traffic in deep waters."
>
> —Archibald MacMechan, 1890, Dalhousie English professor 1889–1931

facing page, clockwise from top left: The first university building, Dalhousie College, facing Grand Parade (where Halifax City Hall now stands), 1825. (UA)

Facsimile of the brass plaque on the original cornerstone of Dalhousie College. (UA)

Halifax street plan, including Dal College, 1878. (NSA)

Silver trowel used by the Earl of Dalhousie to lay the cornerstone, 1820. (NP/UA)

above: Campus plan by Halifax architect Andrew R. Cobb, *Alumni News*, March 1924. (UA)

right: University Avenue, Halifax, captured at dawn in Dal's 200th Anniversary Video. (SS)

The McCulloch Gateway, honoring the memory of Dalhousie's first President, is now a reality and stands at the Coburg Road end of the roadway leading to the Arts and Administration Building. Part of the gateway was erected by the Class of 1918 and the project was completed by a large number of Alumni, mostly senior Dalhousians.

left: *Alumni News*, November 1955. (UA)

"Seeds are planted, truly, in the textbooks and classrooms, but providing space for these seeds to grow, to be nurtured, to cross-pollinate, to thrive, is where real education begins...to create lasting friendships and memories.... This is where education will really bloom."

—Margaret McCain, opening the Wallace McCain Learning Commons, 2015

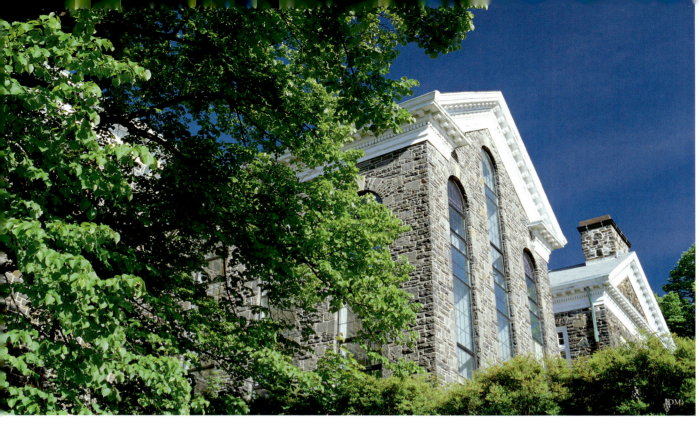

"Here in Nova Scotia, at Dalhousie, is where my ideas have flowered."

—Essy Baniassad, former Dean of Architecture, 2016

clockwise from facing page: Arthur Lismer, a founding member of the Group of Seven, was commissioned to produce drawings such as this one of the Forrest Building for Dalhousie's 100th anniversary in 1919. The building was known as the "New Dalhousie Building" when the university moved from the Grand Parade to the Carleton campus location in 1887. These drawings were advertised as "a complete set of twenty-six copy etchings, suitable for framing, all for One Dollar." (UA)

Studley campus, looking toward First Baptist Church on Oxford Street, 1959. (UA)

Studley Quad, from Alumni Crescent, 1999. (DA)

The *Dalhousie Gazette*, February 1911, reported on the Board's decision to buy land on the Halifax peninsula for $50,000, from Elizabeth Murray (née Carey), widow of former Board member Robert Murray. (UA)

The Agriculture campus at Bible Hill, 1931. (AA)

(NP)

"We're not only gaining a new faculty at Dal — we're adding more than 1,000 unique and innovative students, a dedicated and talented team of professors and employees, and 100 years of tradition. The Nova Scotia Agricultural College is a special place for so many people, and as the Faculty of Agriculture, it will have a special and important place within Dalhousie."

— Dr. Tom Traves, 10th president of Dalhousie, upon the amalgamation of NSAC with Dal, July 1, 2012

The Nova Scotia Agricultural College (NSAC) opened in Bible Hill, near Truro, in 1905. (AA)

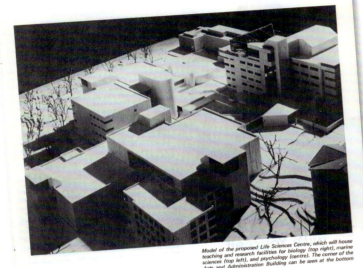

Model of the proposed Life Sciences Centre, which will house teaching and research facilities for biology (top right), marine sciences (top left), and psychology (centre). The corner of the Arts and Administration Building can be seen at the bottom right hand corner.

clockwise from above: Dalhousie Medicine New Brunswick in Saint John, established 2008. (DU)

Model of the proposed Life Sciences Centre published in *Alumni News*, September 1969. (UA)

Collaborative Health Education Building, Carleton campus, opened in 2015. (NP)

Sexton campus, 2014. (NP)

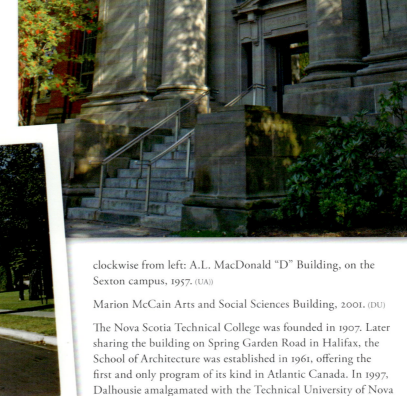

clockwise from left: A.L. MacDonald "D" Building, on the Sexton campus, 1957. (UA)

Marion McCain Arts and Social Sciences Building, 2001. (DU)

The Nova Scotia Technical College was founded in 1907. Later sharing the building on Spring Garden Road in Halifax, the School of Architecture was established in 1961, offering the first and only program of its kind in Atlantic Canada. In 1997, Dalhousie amalgamated with the Technical University of Nova Scotia (TUNS), formerly the Nova Scotia Technical College. (DU)

Henry Hicks Building. (DA)

clockwise from left: Sir James Dunn Building. (DU)

Life Sciences Centre. (NP)

Kenneth C. Rowe Management Building. (NP)

Mona Campbell Building. (DA)

The view in 1999 of what is now the Goldberg Computer Science Building. (DU)

Engineering Building at the corner of Coburg Road and Oxford Street in Halifax, 1957. (HA)

clockwise from above: The Sir Charles Tupper Medical Building in 1967 and the academic gown The Queen Mother wore to receive her honorary doctorate, and officially open the building. (NP/UA)

The renovated Student Union Building opened in 2017 to serve nearly 19,000 students. (Lydon Lynch Architects/Julian Parkinson)

Dal had only 4,500 students when the Student Union Building first opened its doors in 1968. (UA)

Students published the *Dalhousian* in 1914 as part of a fundraising campaign for a new students' building. (UA)

clockwise from right: President Tom Traves (right) and donor Ken Rowe (left) during construction of the Kenneth C. Rowe Management Building, 2005. (DA)

Seymour Schulich, shown here, donated $20 million in 2010, which was, at the time, the largest gift made to a Canadian law school. (DA)

The Steele Ocean Sciences Building, named to honour Harry Steele, was added to the west end of the Life Sciences Centre in 2013. (NP)

"[Donors make] an investment in the Dalhousie community, which represents the faith in the ability for this institution to instill values of generosity, of kindness, and of goodwill in our students."

—Dan Nicholson, Student Union president, 2014–2015

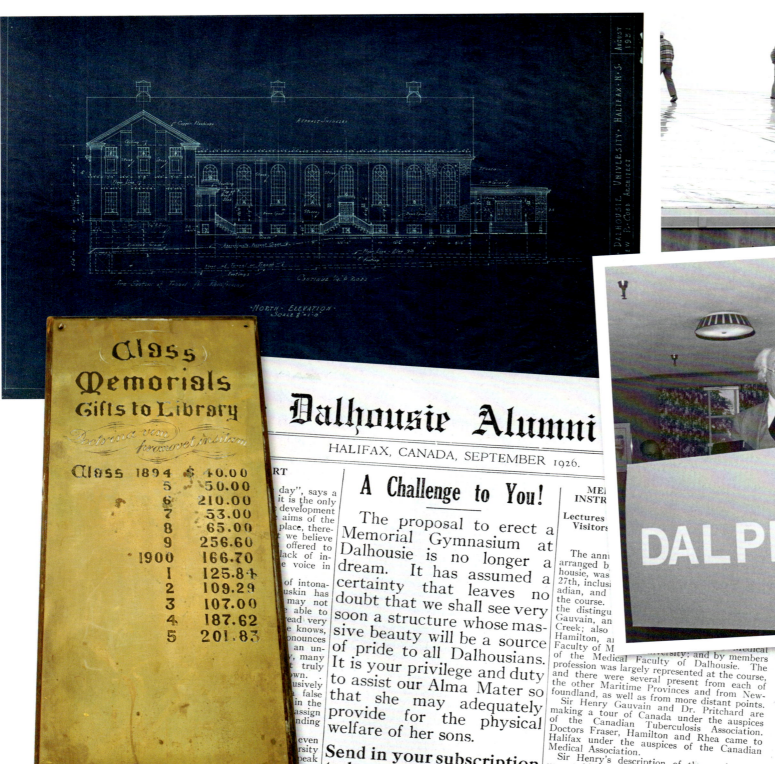

clockwise from top left: Blueprint for Studley Gymnasium by Andrew R. Cobb, 1931. (HA)

After years of planning, Dalplex, the university's recreation facility, opened in 1979 with an innovative "air structure" roof. (UA)

President Henry Hicks speaking at the Dalplex Campaign kick-off, October 13, 1977. (UA)

above: Dalhousie's Memorial Arena was built in 1950 but was destroyed by fire in 1978. The new arena opened in 1982. (NP)

inset: President MacKay and Hockey Coach Peter Esdale with a model of the new arena. (UA)

left: Architects' rendering of the new fitness centre set to open in 2018. (FBM/MJMA)

"Whether you're a student, graduate, faculty, staff, lecturer, administrator—we hope you'll be always proud of your association with the Fountain School of Performing Arts at Dalhousie University. Thank you to all the performers for giving us the opportunity to see you shine."

—Elizabeth Fountain, October 17, 2013

In 2013, Dal's Departments of Music and Theatre merged to form the Fountain School of Performing Arts (FSPA), housed in the Dal Arts Centre (top) and made possible by a $10 million gift from the Fountain family—the largest ever received by the Faculty of Arts and Social Sciences (FASS). (DM)

above: Donors Fred and Elizabeth Fountain, at the naming of the new Fountain School of Performing Arts, October 17, 2013. (NP)

right: Architect's drawing of the proposed expansion to the Dal Arts Centre.

(Lyndon Lynch Thomas Payne Architects)

"I knew something big was going to happen, but I never dreamed it would be this big. I only wish that John could be here to witness the joy and share in this dream come true."

— Marjorie Lindsay (LLD 2016), above, donor and honorary Chair of the IDEA campaign, on her gift to the project to honour her late husband, John Lindsay Sr. (BEng 1951 [NSTC]; DEng 1991)

right: Architects' plans for the new Design Building, part of the IDEA (Innovation and Design in Engineering and Architecture) Project, a transformational investment in the downtown Sexton campus, which will become the engine of Halifax's emerging innovation district. (DSRA Architecture Inc.)

(BB)

# A YEAR IN THE LIFE

University communities are bound to the calendar year in ways that few others are. Events and ceremonies return according to their seasons, to usher in new Dalhousians, to celebrate their successes, to welcome them back, and to launch them into new adventures. The university's rhythms unite faculty, students, staff, and alumni.

The academic year begins in the fall. More than spring, autumn signals our fresh start. The first day of classes rings in our New Year's Day. Winter carries the full intensity of the workload for staff, students, and faculty. In the Maritimes, the cycle of rain and snow, freeze and thaw can make the winter term even more challenging. Spring brings a sense of achievement and the promise of the restorative summer to come.

Interwoven with the seasons' transitions is the ceremonial life of the campus: the inductions, convocations, and awards, even the ritual of examinations. Celebrations punctuate our time together: parties, Mawio'mi, homecoming, and reunions. The familiar cycle of the academic year measures out the life of the university and our years within it.

"What more delightful city than this, wrapped around on all sides by the sea, in which to spend one's student days?"

— R.C. Weldon, Dean of Law, convocation address, October 30, 1883

(BS)

clockwise from left: Lucy Maud Montgomery's signature in the 1895 registration book. Her third book, *Anne of the Island*, was based on her experiences while at Dalhousie. (UA)

Students registering, 1970. (UA)

New science students, September 1965. (UA)

Robert Stanfield's 1932 registration. Stanfield became the 17th premier of Nova Scotia and later the leader of the federal Progressive Conservative Party. (NP/UA)

# Dalhousie University

I hereby apply to be enregistered in Dalhousie University, subject to all the terms laid down in the current Calendar, and agree to be governed by all the Regulations therein, and to payment of the fees, deposits already made. I submit the following facts:

NAME .....Robert Lorne Stanfield.....
(Write each name in full, underlining the Christian name by which you are called)

1. DATE ....Sept. 27, 1932....

HOME ADDRESS ....431 Prince St., Truro, N.S.....

HALIFAX ADDRESS ....122 Edward St.....

PLACE AND DATE OF BIRTH ....April 11, 1914, Truro, N.S.....
(Give month, day and year)

PARENT OR GUARDIAN ....Mrs. Frank Stanfield....

NATIONALITY AND OCCUPATION ....Canadian....

DENOMINATION ....Anglican....

"This is where no matter how different you are, how average you are…you fit. Dal is like a 19,000-piece puzzle and it wouldn't be the same without each and every student. We all fit together, we hold each other up, and we hold each other in place."

—Kelsey Keddy, Dalhousie Student Union vice-president of Student Life, 2016

clockwise from above: Class of 1945 pin. (NP/UA)

The incoming class, October 1892. (UA)

Class of 2020 gathered for their September Induction Ceremony. (DA)

Pharmacy White Coat Ceremony, 2016. (DA)

above: O-week (Orientation) activities in the Studley Quad, 2011. (NP)

top right: Athletic and intramural information advertised during O-Week, 1974. (UA)

bottom right: Of Dal's students, 52 per cent come from out of province, the highest percentage of any university in Canada. (NP)

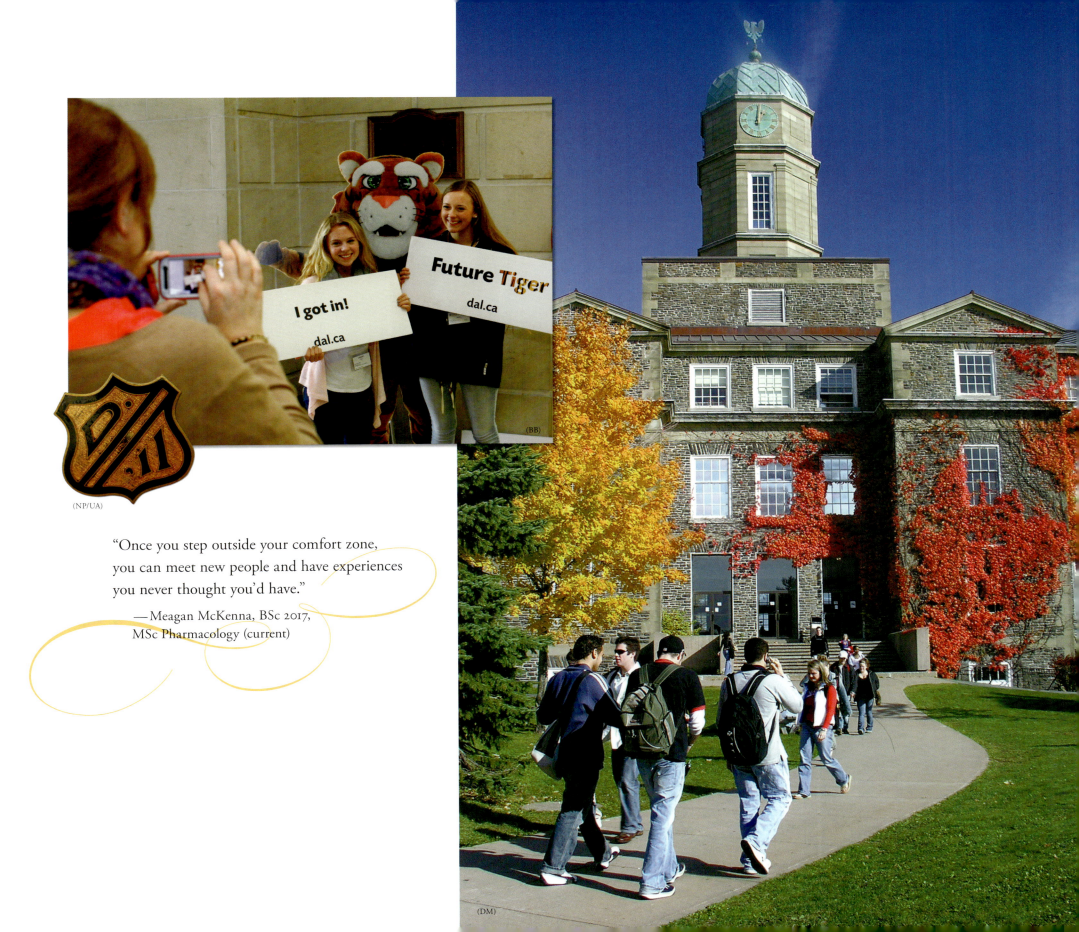

"Once you step outside your comfort zone, you can meet new people and have experiences you never thought you'd have."

— Meagan McKenna, BSc 2017,
MSc Pharmacology (current)

"Building a culture grounded in diversity and inclusiveness is a top priority for Dalhousie.... 'Respect Week' is one of the ways we can encourage understanding and discussion around the experiences of all members of our community."

—Janice MacInnis, manager, Organizational Health, 2015

right: In 2015, Dalhousie expanded "Pink Shirt" day into a full "Respect Week" now held on Dalhousie's campuses each September. (BB)

facing page: Colour Fest, first celebrated on campus in 2015, replicates one of the major festivals of India, known as Holi, representing unity and diversity. The core values of the festival are to spread love and joy among all people, putting aside religion and nationality. (PF)

(NP)

"It goes much deeper than what the eye can see. *Why* we dance has a story.... It is a time to learn and share."

—Chief Gerard Julien, co-chair of the Assembly of Nova Scotia Mi'kmaq Chiefs, 2012

"The Mawio'mi is meant as a welcome, as a means of prayer and healing, and also to foster a sense of community for Aboriginal students on campus. At the same time, you don't have to be Aboriginal to join in; all are welcome. Aboriginal culture is really Canadian culture. It's a celebration for all of us, and it is just a really fun event. Everyone always feels great after a powwow."

—Kara Paul, coordinator of the Dalhousie Aboriginal Health Sciences Initiative, 2010

"I hope that people see the importance of this event for our communties and for the relationship that Dalhousie is working on from the larger picture of reconciliation."

—Michele Graveline, Indigenous student advisor, 2017

Started in 2010 by Indigenous students, Dal's Mawio'mi, or "gathering," is now a highlight of the fall to celebrate and honour Mi'kmaq History Month and raise awareness about Indigenous culture at the University, which sits on traditional Mi'kmaq territory. (DA)

"When the hills beyond the Arm are again clothed in yellow and purple and gold, another year will call itself Senior, and you will have passed from college halls out into the highways of the world. You will still, however, be part of Dalhousie, bound to her and bound to one another by ties that can never break, the memories of four years of youth and hope and ambition. The college will still call you her own and look with pride on you as you go forth bearing her name."

—G.E. Wilson, honorary president, Class of 1927

facing page left: Dal seen from the Northwest Arm. (FM)

facing page top right: Fans attend a Tigers football game, Homecoming 2013. (CP)

facing page bottom right: President's Fun Run, Homecoming 2016. (NP)

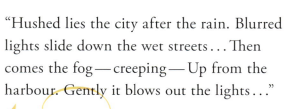

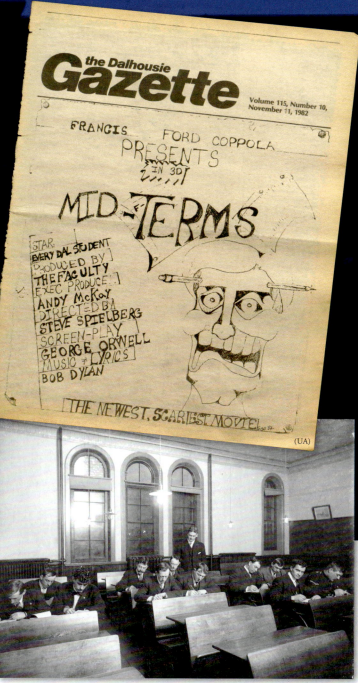

"Hushed lies the city after the rain. Blurred lights slide down the wet streets… Then comes the fog — creeping — Up from the harbour. Gently it blows out the lights…"
— by "Omhpos," *Dalhousie Gazette*, 1948

above: A night class at the Nova Scotia Technical College, ca. 1910. (UA)

top right: The Annual Dalhousie Carol Sing brings together faculty, staff, students, family, and friends for classic carols, holiday, and Hanukkah songs. (NP)

bottom right: The All Nations Drummers offer a traditional welcome to open the festive event. (NP)

clockwise from left: the Puppy Room, instigated by the Dalhousie Students Union in 2012 to relieve exam stress. (DA)

Students check their publicly posted grades, ca. 1950s. (UA)

Exam time in 1990. (BS)

Exams in the Memorial Arena, 1988. (UA)

"The truth about carrying torches is that they get very heavy after a long journey and our journey has been very long. We still have a long way to go. Today we have a torch that is burning brightly because of the hard work of the many people who came before us."

—The Honourable Tony Ince, Minister of Communities, Culture and Heritage and of African Nova Scotian Affairs, at the first flag raising, 2017

Since 2017, February's African Heritage Month includes the raising of the Pan-African Flag. (DA)

clockwise from left: In 2013, Dalhousie inaugurated a new June tradition: the Strawberry Social for staff and faculty. (NP)

Retirees' Reception at the president's residence, 2016. (DA)

Don Laporte, catering manager, is a familiar face on the Halifax campuses since 2005. (DA)

DSU elections in March mark the end of one executive's term of service and the beginning of new student leadership.

top to bottom: Student council class presidents, 1931. (UA)

Rusty James (left), student union vice-president, and Alex Gigeroff, student union president, 1984–1985. (UA)

Amina Abawajy, DSU president 2017–2018. (NP)

Aaron Prosper, DSU president 2018–2019. (NP)

Beginning in 2016, new convocation traditions honour history and heritage: medicine pouches (left) and Kente sashes (below) are now a part of Dal's ceremonies. (NP)

left: Graduate Jacqueline Smith receives her medicine pouch from Elder Geri Musqua-LeBlanc, 2016. (DA)

below: The Governor General's Gold Medal awarded to Frank H. Bell in 1876. (NP/UA)

bottom left: Pen nib used by President Stanley to sign degrees in 1944 and 1945. (NP/UA)

facing page, right: Women graduates, 1905. (UA)

facing page, centre right: Graduates in the Forrest Building, 1892. (UA)

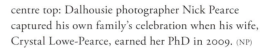

centre top: Dalhousie photographer Nick Pearce captured his own family's celebration when his wife, Crystal Lowe-Pearce, earned her PhD in 2009. (NP)

bottom right: Chancellor Anne McLellan (BA 1971, LLB 1974) and Board Chair Larry Stordy (LLB/MBA 1984) presiding at spring convocation, 2016. (DA)

facing page, inset: Agriculture's official "barley" ring launched in 2010. (NP)

"We are about to leave the old walls which have run so merrily to our voices for the last four years. We are going to leave behind those scenes, the reminiscences of which will continue to spring up so vividly before us in after life.

—Alexander H. McKay, valedictory speech, May 3, 1873

(UA)

# 3 QUEST FOR KNOWLEDGE

"A [student]...should go [to university]—to prepare herself for living; not alone in the finite but in the infinite. She goes to have her mind broadened and her powers of observation cultivated. She goes to study her own race in all the bewildering perplexities of its being. In short, she goes to find out the best, easiest and most effective way of living the life that God and nature planned out for her to live."

— Lucy Maud Montgomery, from "A Girl's Place at Dalhousie College," *Halifax Herald*, 1896

The search for knowledge lies at the very heart of a university. At Dalhousie, research and teaching are inextricably linked. Both are guided by the pursuit of excellence. This holds as true for staff and administrators and donors—all of whom play a role in this noble endeavour—as it does for the professors and students working together daily. All the diverse sources of support help to make this important work possible.

The process of discovering and sharing knowledge can be infinitely varied and abstract, or focused and concrete. In cultivating an environment for rigorous inquiry, Dalhousie has served as home to internationally recognized professors and world-class students. The images that follow capture some of those moments of discovery. Dal's teaching and research have looked very different in the past, and they will continue to evolve with the expanding frontiers of knowledge.

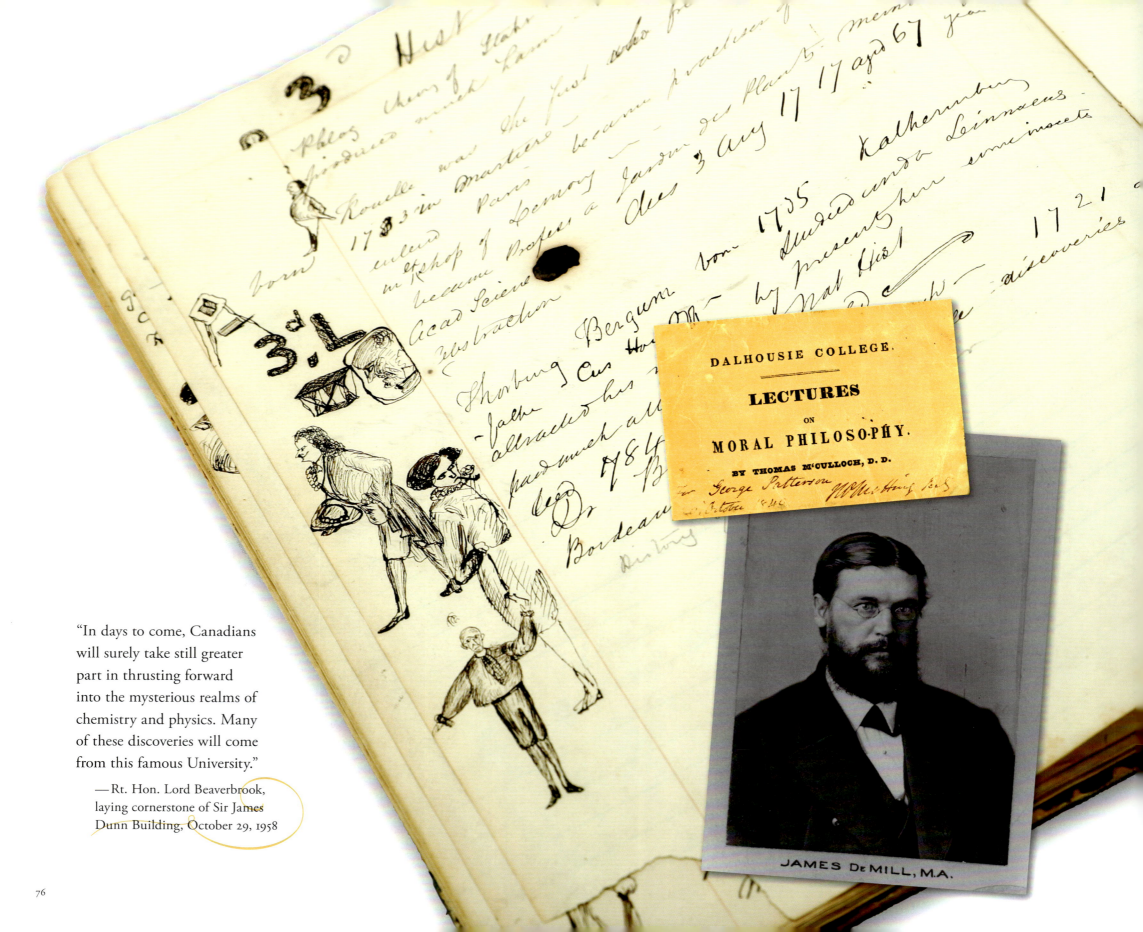

"In days to come, Canadians will surely take still greater part in thrusting forward into the mysterious realms of chemistry and physics. Many of these discoveries will come from this famous University."

—Rt. Hon. Lord Beaverbrook, laying cornerstone of Sir James Dunn Building, October 29, 1958

facing page: A ticket for a lecture by Dalhousie's 1st president, Dr. Rev. Thomas McCulloch, hand-dated October 1840. (NP/UA)

The Department of English, one of the oldest in Canada, was founded with the appointment of James De Mille as the first professor of rhetoric, from 1865 to 1880. (UA)

De Mille's own student notebooks with notes for "3rd History Lecture." (NP/UA)

right: Leitz compound microscope, 1910. (NP/TM)

top right: Engineering student Bai Bintou Kaira, 2017 president of the Dalhousie African Student Association and mentor with Imhotep's Legacy Academy since 2014 (see page 90). (NP)

facing page, top left: Geology field school, 2016. (NP)

top right: Students at the Nova Scotia Technical College, 1924. (UA)

bottom left: A maquette for the stage production of *The Decameron*, 2014. (NP/FSPA)

below left: Third-year student working in Dal's dentistry labs, 2016. (NP)

below right: Tools of the trade for Dentistry students from the turn of the last century. (NP/DD)

"We are so lucky to be at a place where the sky is the limit."

—Sarah Tremaine, third-year Medicine student, 2017

"The Liberal Education is something different.... It is a discipline of mind.... It is not information but cultivation."

—Professor James De Mille, inaugural address, November 4, 1873

facing page, inset: Latin class, 1910, a requirement at Dal until 1956. (UA)

far right: A virtual reality exhibition at the Dalhousie Art Gallery, 2017. (WJ)

below: Installation of a nuclear magnetic resonance machine for the Faculty of Engineering, 2003. (FM)

below right: Stereoscope for studying anatomy slides, ca. 1860s. (NP/MA)

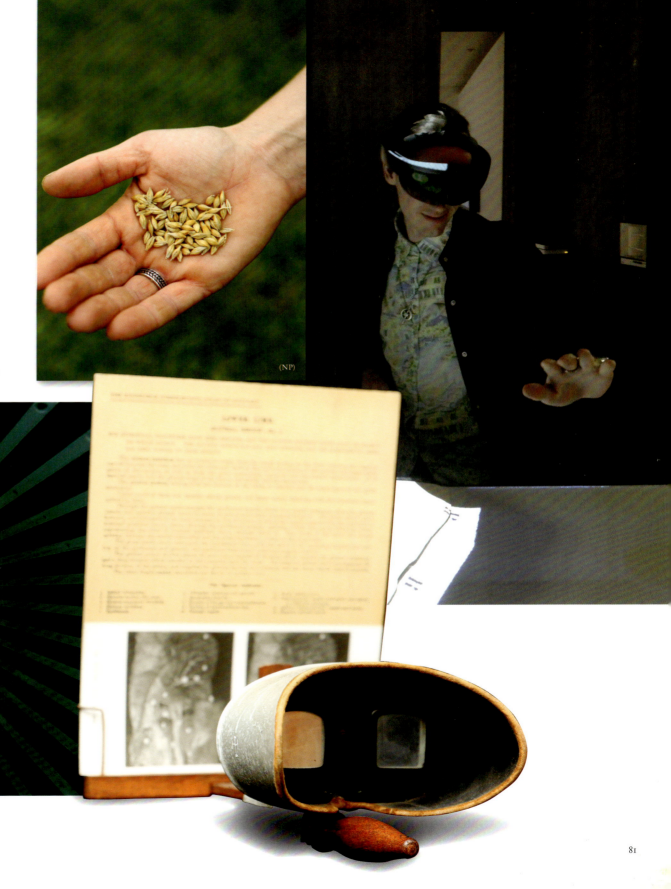

"You must not only set yourselves free by learning the truth, you must help to set others free."

—President Carleton Stanley, address to freshmen, September 24, 1931

above: Medical Computer Centre, 1970. (UA)

right: In 1964, Dalhousie's first computer, an IBM 1620, had to be hoisted by crane into the upper floor of the Dunn Building. (UA)

inset: Dalhousie adopted Brightspace in 2015, a system that allows students and professors to manage coursework from their hand-held devices. (RF)

top right: MacDonald Memorial Library, 1930s. (UA)

right: Dalhousie's Killam Memorial Library, opened in 1971, is the largest academic library in Atlantic Canada. (NP)

left: Lecture hall, 1980s. (BS)

top: Artist Dana Claxton's *Mustang Suite*, at the Dalhousie Art Gallery, 2017, acquired through the generosity of alumni of the Schulich School of Law. (WJ)

facing page inset: Returning WWII Veterans fill an English class in 1945. (UA)

(PM)

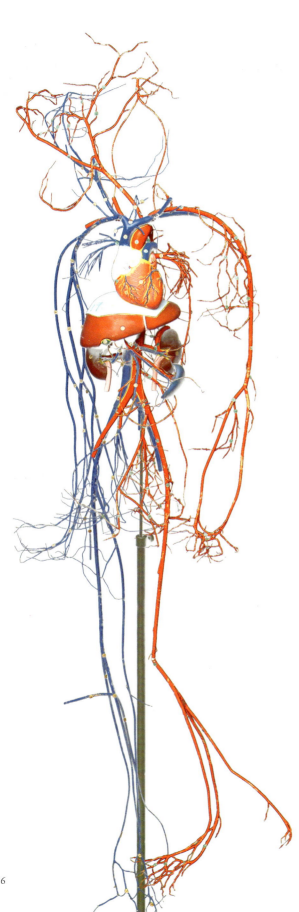

"Here the shy learn to assert themselves; the conceited get quick and salutary lessons of modesty; the dogmatic find there are other opinions besides their own."

—Charles A. MacDonald, Professor of Mathematics, 1870

clockwise from left: Model of the human circulatory system, in the R.L. de C.H. Saunders Museum of Anatomy. (NP/MA)

Dal Architecture students at work, Ross Creek, 2010. (NP)

Experiment in the Sir James Dunn Building, ca. 1950s. (UA)

Costume design for Dal's Theatre Department's 1995 production of *Red Noses*. Dalhousie's Costume Studies program is the only one of its kind in Canada. (UA)

top to bottom: Anatomy lab in the Forrest Building, ca. 1890s. (MA)

Running an experiment, ca. 1968. (UA)

Anatomy lab in the Sir Charles Tupper Medical Building, 2007. (MA)

(PM)

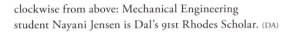

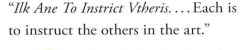

clockwise from above: Mechanical Engineering student Nayani Jensen is Dal's 91st Rhodes Scholar. (DA)

Dalhousie's first Rhodes Scholar, Gilbert S. Stairs (BA 1903). (UA)

Professor Axel Becke is one of the most referenced researchers in the world. Two of his articles rank among the top twenty-five most-cited papers of all time, across all disciplines. (NSERC)

Molecular biologist Ford Doolittle was the first Atlantic Canadian to receive the Gerhard Herzberg Canada Gold Medal for Science and Engineering. The Herzberg Medal, recognizing research excellence and influence, was named in honour of Canada's 1971 Nobel prize winner in Chemistry, and includes a $1 million research grant. (DA)

The Herzberg Medal is considered Canada's most prestigious scientific research prize. It has been won by Dal professors in three of the last four years. In 2015 it was awarded to Axel Becke and the 2017 winner was Prof. Jeff Dahn (see page 91).

Alumnus Arthur McDonald (BSc 1964, MSc 1965), co-winner of the 2015 Nobel Prize in Physics, speaking to a packed house at Dal in 2017. (DA)

The crest in the floor of the Sir Charles Tupper Medical Building features a healing pine cone from the Tree of Life according to the *Dalhousie Medical Journal*, 1954. (NP)

The Silver Shovel Award celebrates medical school professors who show outstanding compassion and commitment to students. The shovel itself was used to break ground on the Tupper building in 1965. (NP)

*"Ilk Ane To Instrict Vtheris.... Each is to instruct the others in the art."*

— Motto of the Dalhousie Medical Students' Society

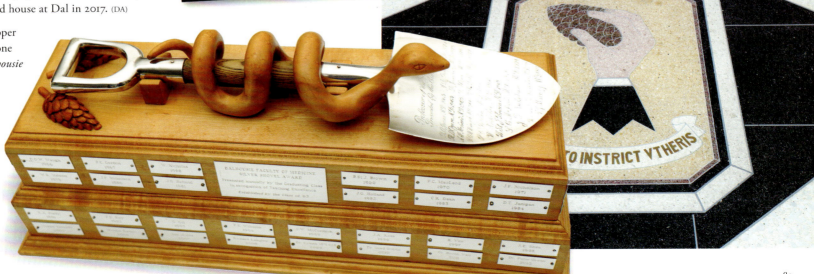

left: Founded by Dal's Chair of Senate, Dr. Kevin Hewitt, Imhotep's Legacy Academy brings African Nova Scotian students together with university mentors to increase the representation of African Canadians in Science, Technology, Engineering, and Math professions. (SI)

below: Sean Myles, Canada Research Chair in Agricultural Genetic Diversity, and his eight-person lab focus on preserving the biodiversity of apple varieties. (BB)

left: Dal's Ocean Frontier Institute (OFI) one of the world's most significant international ocean science collaborations was formed in 2016 with the announcement of over $200 million in federal, provincial, and partner funding—including a $25 million gift from business leader and philanthropist John Risley, an unprecedented investment in Canada's ocean science sector and the largest research grant in Dal's history. (iSP)

facing page: The Ocean Tracking Network, headquartered at Dalhousie, is a collaboration with over one hundred research institutions worldwide, tracking the movements and survival of aquatic animals globally since 2008. (SK)

facing page, inset: Jeff Dahn's team working on lithium-ion batteries are international leaders in advanced materials and clean technology. In 2015, Dalhousie was the only university to partner with Tesla in the fight against climate change. (NP)

"My grandfather fished this ocean almost 100 years ago, and today I plumb its depths for knowledge. Partnering with Dalhousie just made sense—but we had to get over history and recognize the need for a different way of working together. One ocean, one institute, one excellent team."

—Dr. Paul Snelgrove, Memorial University, on OFI, 2017

"You can see a trajectory…leading up to this day. I think the ancestors are proud, they are pleased, they are happy. We will continue to do the work that is necessary to make diversity and inclusiveness a reality at Dalhousie."

—Dr. Afua Cooper, James R. Johnston Chair in Black Canadian Studies and founder of the Black Canadian Studies Association, 2017

facing page, top: In 2013, Dal launched a new minor in Popular Culture Studies. (DA)

facing page: Dr. Afua Cooper, coordinator of the new minor in Black and African Diaspora Studies launched in 2016. (DA)

facing page, inset: In 1995, Patricia Doyle-Bedwell became the first Indigenous faculty member at Dalhousie. (DA)

right: In 2016, Schulich School of Law professor Naiomi Metallic was named Dal's first Chancellor's Chair in Aboriginal Law and Policy. The Chair was made possible through a generous donation by the Honourable Anne McLellan, Dal's 7th chancellor. (RK)

below: Annual FASS Publication and Performance Launch.

"Dalhousie has important things to say, to do, to teach, to publish."

—P.B. Waite, Emeritus Professor of History, 1990

above: James Robinson Johnston was the first African Nova Scotian to graduate from Dalhousie Law School in 1898. Now Dal sponsors the James R. Johnston Chair in Black Canadian Studies to bring Black culture, experiences, and concerns into the academy. (NSA)

# 4 DAL IN THE WORLD

"There's no question I came out of Dal with a strong sense of wanting to do something with my life and in the world."

—Jim Spatz (MD 1974) endowed a Chair in Jewish Studies in honour of his parents, Holocaust survivors Simon and Riva Spatz, and in recognition that Dalhousie, unlike other universities, never had a quota on the number of Jewish students it would accept.

Any university that aspires to be world-class has a threefold mission. Along with teaching and research, Dalhousie is founded upon service: the commitment to ensure that research has benefit and that Dal citizens are making a difference in the world. The reach of this service extends well beyond Dal's five university campuses through the work of students, faculty, staff, and alumni in the community and around the world. Our pursuit of academic excellence reverberates in the social, cultural, and economic life of our city, our region, our country, and our world.

Much of the meaning of a university in society is enacted outside the classroom, in the lives of its various communities, whether local or international. The images here evoke some of Dalhousie's successes and also our shared commitment to translate those successes toward making a better world.

left: After completing her PhD at Dal, Dr. Kathryn Sullivan became one of the first six women ever admitted to NASA's astronaut corps. In 1984, she became the first American woman to walk in space. (DR)

below: Barbara Hinds, a public relations expert and medical reporter for the Dal Faculty of Medicine, travelling on the Koksoak River, Nunavik, 1960. (UA)

page 94: Dr. Anna Metaxas and Dr. Robert Scheibling collaborate with colleagues at Ben-Gurion University in Israel to conserve coral reefs in the Red Sea. (RS)

page 95: Tony Pesklevits, Master of Environmental Studies student, in the old growth stand at Panuke Lake, NS, 2007. (RO)

"Dalhousie is open, with all its privileges, to any lady capable of entering."
— Board of Governors, 1881, making Dal the first Canadian university to admit women with equal access to scholarships and awards

A.W. THOMPSON   K.J. MARTIN   O.G. CAMPBELL   J.M. McLEOD   A. STANLEY MACKENZIE   H.H.K. FITZPATRICK
R. M. LANGILLE   W.M. TUFFTS   MARGARET F. NEWCOMBE   I. GAMMELL   F.S. COFFIN
W. AITON   R.T. LOCKE   G.E. ROBINSON

SENIOR CLASS, '85.
DALHOUSIE COLLEGE.

"I think it's safe to say, most of us have very similar long-term aspirations for the place we call home.... I believe we all have a responsibility to try to make a difference in our region, now and into the future."

—Bob Hanf, vice-chair, Dalhousie Board of Governors (LLB 1989)

above: In 1885, Margaret Florence Newcombe was awarded her BA and became the first woman to graduate from Dalhousie. (UA)

top right: In 1919, Eliza Ritchie (BA 1887) was appointed to the Dalhousie Board of Governors, making her the first woman in Canada to hold such a position. (UA)

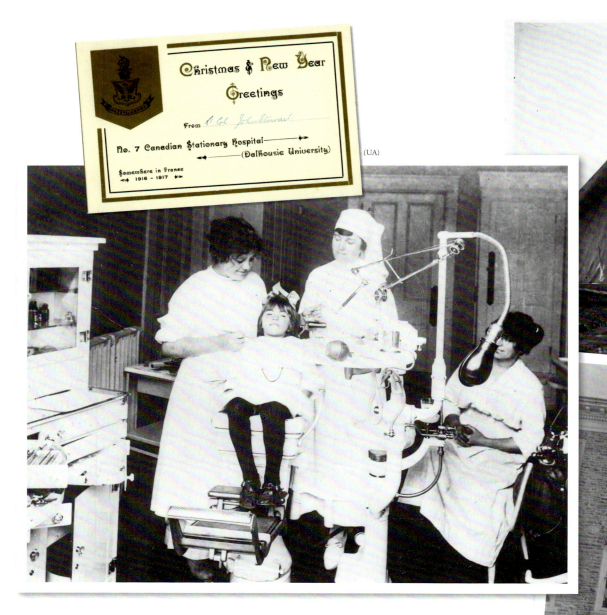

"Within fifteen minutes after the explosion, probably every student in the higher three years was rendering first aid, and the majority of students from every faculty were assisting in a variety of ways as numerous as the needs they saw.... Suffice it to say that the majority of Dalhousians responded with true Dalhousie spirit to the needs of their suffering fellows."

— *Dalhousie Gazette*, January 29, 1918

above: During the First World War, the No. 7 Hospital formed to treat Canadian soldiers at the front. Its 162 medical personnel were all students and professors from the Dalhousie Medical School. (UA)

left: Windows in the science building and library, damaged in the 1917 Halifax Explosion. (UA)

far left: Dr. Arabelle MacKenzie, first woman dental graduate of Dalhousie, at the pre-school dental clinic she established in 1918, following the Halifax Explosion. (UA)

far right: Pilot Officer W. Rand Lugar was the first Dalhousie student to be killed in the Second World War. (UA)

centre bottom: This Second World War era medical briefcase made out of brass, housed in the Dal Archives, bears initials MGH. (NP/UA)

"The question of questions today is whether tyranny and despotism are going to spread and engulf the world, or whether liberty will find, here and there, a citadel.... If there be no freedom, there cannot really be universities, so for their self-preservation, the universities must stand for freedom."

— President Carleton Stanley, at annual closing, May 15, 1935

above: Agricultural College open house, 1973. (AA)

right: For over fifty years, Dal students have shined shoes, washed cars, and sung songs for Shinerama, raising money for cystic fibrosis research. (DA)

bottom: Commerce students' 5 Days for the Homeless campaign, 2017. (DA)

"There is a world of wonders out there that you really have to experience first-hand in order to appreciate it, and volunteering is a great way to do that. Whether you make a big difference, or just change one life, what you give cannot begin to compare with the feeling of fulfillment you get from it."

—Glenn Dodge, (BComm 1991, LLB 1994), 2016 Dalhousie Alumni Association Volunteerism Award honoree

**Dal champions the United Way** (UA)

above: November 1983 issue of *Dal News* reports Dalhousie's contribution to the United Way, now a yearly campaign. (UA)

facing page, inset left: The Faculty of Agriculture, led by Rocky the Ram, joins the Town of Truro's first Pride Parade in 2016. (NP)

"The University of North Preston was where I discovered myself and it was the foundation for my engagement with the community."

—Dr. Amid Ismail, co-founder of the North Preston Dental Clinic, a collaboration between the Faculty of Dentistry and the North Preston community

above: The third-year Medicine Class of 1937 on the steps of the Public Health Clinic. (UA)

right: Burnley (Rocky) Jones (LLB 1992, LLD 2004), here in 2011, realized as an undergraduate that "there must be something blocking First Nations and African Nova Scotians from getting through." In 1969, he co-founded the Transition Year Program (TYP) (far right), unique in Canada, to help Black and Indigenous students attain the skills they needed to get a university education. Since its inception, more than one thousand people have graduated from TYP. (UA)

facing page: Maria Dugas, LLM student, 2016. The law school established the Indigenous Blacks and Mi'kmaq Initiative (IB&M) program in 1989, ensuring that Mi'kmaq and African Nova Scotian students have equitable representation in the law school—and in the justice system. (DA)

facing page inset: In 1970, Dalhousie Legal Aid began as the first legal service for Nova Scotia's low-income community. It is now the oldest clinical law program in Canada. (RK)

"Dal Theatre explores our human longing to refashion ourselves and our world, in the hope that change can be for the better."

—Fountain School of the Performing Arts, 2017–2018 program

(NP)

Plate 1. 'IN' BUT NOT 'OF' THE CITY. Africville (along the shoreline), as shown in this picture, was relatively isolated from the rest of the City of Halifax.
—Bob Brooks Photo

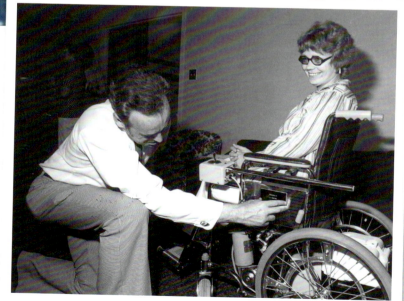

"Universities have a role to play in developing the great human potential of all our communities.... I truly believe that no one achieves anything alone and that's as true for institutions and communities as it is for individuals. Look what we can do when we bring the best of our region together with the best of the world, when we find ways to be more inclusive, when we challenge ourselves to think bigger."

—President Richard Florizone, to the Halifax Chamber of Commerce, 2016

top: The *Africville Relocation Report* of 1971, by Don Clairmont and Dennis Magill of Dal's Institute of Public Affairs, documented the story of the residents whose homes and lands were expropriated by the City of Halifax during the 1960s. (KL)

left: Andrew MacKay, Dalhousie's 8th president, places a commemorative plaque on Donna Crawford's new power wheelchair, purchased for her with funds from the Dalhousie community, 1976. (UA)

facing page: The Blanket Exercise fosters understanding of how colonization impacted Indigenous peoples. Blankets represent the land, and participants walk through re-imagined phases of pre-contact, treaty making, colonization, and resistance. (NP)

facing page, inset: In 2003, DalOUT began offering education, support, and network-building for the LGBTQ+ community in Nova Scotia. (DA)

"It makes my heart smile seeing so many faculty and staff attend the Blanket Exercise. When the administration of an institution involves itself in learning controversial history, it tells me that they are committed to moving toward reconciliation."

— Elder Geri Musqua-LeBlanc

"The modern university must not withdraw itself from contemporary society."

—President Henry Hicks, inaugural address, 1963

above: In 1979, the Dalhousie Medical School hosted a television show to raise awareness about sexual issues, called "Let's Talk about Sex." (UA)

bottom: Dalhousie became the first smoke-free campus in Canada in 2003. (RM)

Chaka Walls, of the Black Panther Party, addressed a group of one thousand students at Dal, February 1970. (CH)

In 2002, the Faculty of Agriculture established the 2+2 BSc program with Fujian University. The program welcomes Chinese students to Nova Scotia for the final two years of their degree. (DA)

clockwise from above: In 2016, Dal hosted a citizenship ceremony for new Canadians. (DA)

Dal is ranked as one of the most international universities in the world. (NP)

Computer science students and the Syrian Student Society hosted a programming camp for newcomers. (AH)

In 2012, German chancellor Angela Merkel, pictured here with Prof. Boris Worme and President Tom Traves, visited Dalhousie to sign a memo of understanding between the Halifax Marine Research Institute and Germany's Helmholtz Association to support ocean research. (DA)

clockwise from left: In 2016, Wanda Thomas Bernard became the first African Nova Scotian woman to hold a tenure track position at Dalhousie University, to be promoted to full professor, and, in 2017, to be appointed to Canada's Senate. (NP)

Alexa McDonough (BA 1965, MSW 1969, LLD 2009) became the first woman in Canada to lead a recognized political party when she was chosen as leader of the Nova Scotia New Democratic Party in 1980. She also led the federal NDP from 1995 to 2003. (DA)

Alumnus R.B. Bennett (LLB 1893) became prime minister of Canada in 1930. (US)

The editor of the *Alumni News* 1971 had it wrong: along with Dal grads Richard Hatfield (1956), premier of New Brunswick 1970–1987; Gerald Regan (1952), premier of Nova Scotia 1970–1978; and Alex B. Campbell (1959), premier of Prince Edward Island 1966–1978, Dal grad and Rhodes Scholar Allan Blakeney (1947) was the premier of Saskatchewan 1971–1982. (UA)

Bertha Wilson (LLB 1957) became the first female Justice of the Supreme Court of Canada in 1982. (UA)

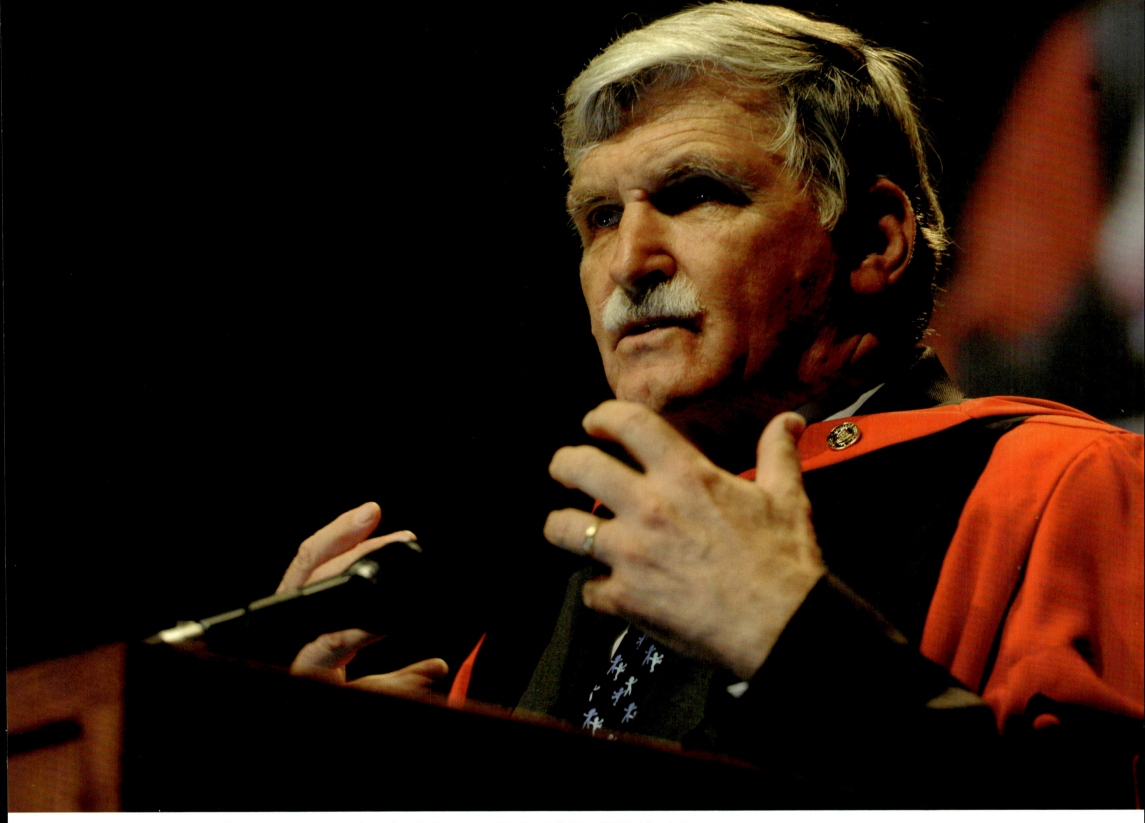

Lieutenant-General Roméo Dallaire receiving an honorary degree from Dalhousie, 2012. The Roméo Dallaire Child Soldiers Initiative, housed at Dalhousie since 2010, seeks to end the use of child soldiers through research, advocacy, and education. (DA)

# 5 YOU WERE HERE

"I don't know where I'd be if it wasn't for Dalhousie. This place has made everything in my life to date possible."

—Chancellor Anne McLellan (BA 1971, LLB 1974), deputy prime minister of Canada 2003–2006

Some of our best memories of university life have nothing to do with our courses and classrooms. Residence and campus life—sports, clubs, performances—are often what first leap to mind when we recall our university days. The objects we hold and treasure, wear and remember, all of this is the "stuff of life." The things we once touched, touch us, assuming a place in our lives.

Most of all, we recall our friendships: teammates, colleagues, roommates. Students remember the classmate who sat beside them long after they've forgotten what exams they studied for. Staff remember their colleague's kind words more than their assigned tasks. Professors remember their students, not the grades they assigned. As our current president, Dr. Richard Florizone, often says, "Nobody does anything alone." You were here. In the life of someone else, that has made all the difference.

clockwise from above: Quoits Club, ca. 1911. (UA)

A meeting of the Tandem Club in front of the original college building, ca. 1825. (UA)

Dalhousie Dramatic Club, with President and Mrs. A.E. Kerr (seated centre), ca. 1959. (UA)

facing page: Kunwardeep Singh (left) and Hasmeet Singh Chandok (right) of the Maritime Bhangra Group — nearly all the members are Dal students or alum. The group's performances of Bhangra, a traditional dance from Punjab, have gained them a viral online following. (DA)

page 112: Studley campus, 1925. (UA)

"A university does not mean buildings or lectures, examinations, and degrees. A university means an atmosphere.... This Temple of Learning shall always be to you, a feasting presence full of light."

—Dr. Devendra Varma, address at Graduation Banquet, May 13, 1964

top right: Dance scene from FSPA's stage production of *The Green Bird*, 2016. (NP)

bottom right: "Homer," renowned resident of the seawater labs, appeared on the cover of *Science Magazine*. (NP/TM)

Facing page: The annual Woodsmen Competition at the Agricultural campus, 2015. (NP)

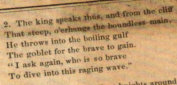

"Dalhousie Student Union: students serving students since 1866"

—T-shirt slogan, ca. 1990s

top: Student band Tiger Patrol, 2013. (BB)

above: CKDU, Dalhousie's community radio station, 1975. (UA)

inset: The Student Union's "Grand Opening of Our Building" mascot from 1968. (UA)

top left: The first issue of the *Dalhousie Gazette*, Canada's first and longest-running college newspaper, January 25, 1869. (UA)

facing page: The *Gazette* offices, 1947. (UA)

"The grand object of this Association be the promotion of the best interests of our University and the fostering of an affection for one another, and for our Alma Mater."

— Dalhousie Alumni Association, 1871 resolution

top to bottom: Dave Slade and Hilda Whittle met while working together at Dalhousie as groundskeeper and custodian. Dave retired during Dal's 200th year. (DA)

From the January 1925 *Dal Gazette*. (UA)

Agricultural College prom, 1947. (AA)

Dance card from Pharmacy Ball, 1963. (MH/PMu)

facing page: Law students' dinner at the Queen Hotel, 1913. (UA)

top: The Shirreff Hall dining room, 1937. (UA)

"Dalhousie is a city university...and has to fight for the attention of its students, amid the distractions (and bars) of the metropolis; but it has engendered its own supporters...and even more important, loyalties in the minds and hearts of students and faculty."

—P.B. Waite, 1990

clockwise from top left: Alpha Gamma Delta–Alpha Eta Chapter sorority pin from 1937 and hand-crafted felt sorority and fraternity figures. (NP/UA)

Phi Delta Theta House, ca. 1989. (BS)

From *Alumni News*, July 1964. (UA)

Dal's rugby team officially adopted the university colours of black and gold in 1887. (UA)

inset: Medicine football team of 1905. (UA)

above: The Tigers won their first Atlantic Football League title in 2016 during the team's 70th anniversary. (MK)

right: This football, signed by the team, is from the 1957 Dal win over Shearwater. (NP/UA)

"Being involved in sport is what drives me to do well in school.... The lessons I've learned—self-discipline, always wanting to improve—I carry those over into the classroom."

—Anna von Maltzahn, a fourth-year neuroscience major and member of cross-country and basketball teams, 2011 (BSc 2013)

left: Adrienne Power is the most decorated Dal Tigers athlete ever: a 2008 Olympian, with 18 AUS wins and 9 CIS medals. (DU)

below: "University Gym Show," 1925. (UA)

The 1982 Tigers women's volleyball team won Canadian Interuniversity Sport championship gold. Not before (or since) has a team from the Atlantic University Sport (AUS) conference captured a national championship in volleyball.

right: Women's volleyball captured their sixth consecutive AUS title in 2018. (NP)

right top: Following an undefeated regular season, the 1995 Tigers men's soccer team became the first Nova Scotia men's soccer team to win the Canadian Interuniversity Sport championship gold. (NP)

above: The men's hockey team, 1911. (UA)

top: For the first time in fifty-two years, the 1979 men's hockey team won the Atlantic University Hockey conference and then went on to take silver in the nationally televised Canadian Interuniversity Sport championship game in Montreal. (UA)

above: In 1976, the Dalhousie varsity field hockey team became the Canadian Intercollegiate Athletic Union champions following an undefeated regular season. (UA)

top: After finishing the 2017 AUS campaign with a third straight conference banner, the men's basketball team took home third place in the national championship—the best finish in team history. (NP)

### Are You Coming To The
### 1926 Convocation and Reunion

| | | |
|---|---|---|
| Sunday May 9th. | 7.00 p.m. | Baccalaureate Sermon. |
| Monday May 10th. | 10.00 a.m. | Buildings Open for Inspection. |
| | 3.00 p.m. | Class Day Exercises |
| | 6.00 p.m. | Alumni Annual Meeting and Dinner at the Green Lantern. |
| | 8.15 p.m. | Students' Play, "The Private Secretary" at the Majestic. |
| Tuesday May 11th. | 10.00 a.m. | Class Reunions. |
| | 3.00 p.m. | Convocation. |
| | 5.00 p.m. | Tea & Reception at Shirreff Hall. |
| | 8.30 p.m. | Convocation Dance. |

Out-of-Town Alumni who intend coming please advise the Secretary, P. O. Box 1017

*A good chance to motor in for the Week End*

clockwise from above: Reunion, 1924. (UA)

Alumni line up for Dalhousie University's centenary parade procession in 1919. (UA)

Alumni reunion, 2010. (DA)

Grads of 1897 gather in 1947 at their 50th reunion. (UA)

top: Celebrating the Dalhousie Centenary in 1919. (UA)

above: One hundred years later, celebrating Dal's 200th anniversary, January 10, 2018. (DU)

top left: Halifax Alumni Chapter at City Hall, 2017. (NP)

above: The first Annual Dinner of the Dalhousie Club of New York, 1931. (UA)

left: Dalhousie College cup and saucer, ca. 1919. (NP/UA)

"We so enjoyed the Dalhousie evening at the Glenbow. It was so special for Mom.... I am not sure if the Dal team has told you, but my Mom died suddenly early Monday morning. For our family, sharing the story of the Dalhousie night last Wednesday evening, has been a wonderful story to share. Thank you for giving Mom this special evening, and that the President's award was to Janet and Graham. Mom was so pleased that you included Dad. The Dal team forwarded several photos from the evening, for us, this one was a treasure."

—letter from Anne Bennett, 2016

President Richard Florizone, wearing the 1944 Dal sweater of Graham Bennett (BSc 1943, BEng 1945) while talking with alumna Janet Bennett (BA 1950), who brought her late husband's sweater and wore her own Dal blazer to the alumni event in Calgary, November 2016, to receive the President's Circle plaque in recognition of donors' lifetime giving. (AN)

# 6 MY DAL

A book like this cannot claim to be comprehensive; you will know more about your own time at Dal than can be captured here. And so, you will fill in the gaps, revisiting your own story as you peruse these pages. The memories represented in this book serve as an invitation to reflect upon the stories — similar and different from your own — the people who went before you, and those who might come after.

This chapter offers an opportunity to continue the story of Dalhousie by adding your own pictures — memories of your time and connections forged here. You have been a part of the grand mission of the university: the research and teaching, the seasons and ceremonies, the outreach and service, the friendships and activities. We invite you to conclude this book, as George Elliott Clarke's poem opens it, by weaving your own story in pictures and mementoes into Dalhousie's 200th anniversary portrait. You are part of a rich history and hopeful mission: loving learning, seeking knowledge, and serving the community. As a citizen of Dal, you have the opportunity to make the world a better place than you found it. See yourself in that bigger picture.

"Being at a university is like falling in love; no one can ever have had such an experience before.... What is it about one's university that colours the whole of the rest of life?... Is it not... the discovery of oneself in relation to the general scheme of things, which was there before us and will outlast us?"

— Sir Walter Langdon-Brown
(Honorary LLD 1938)

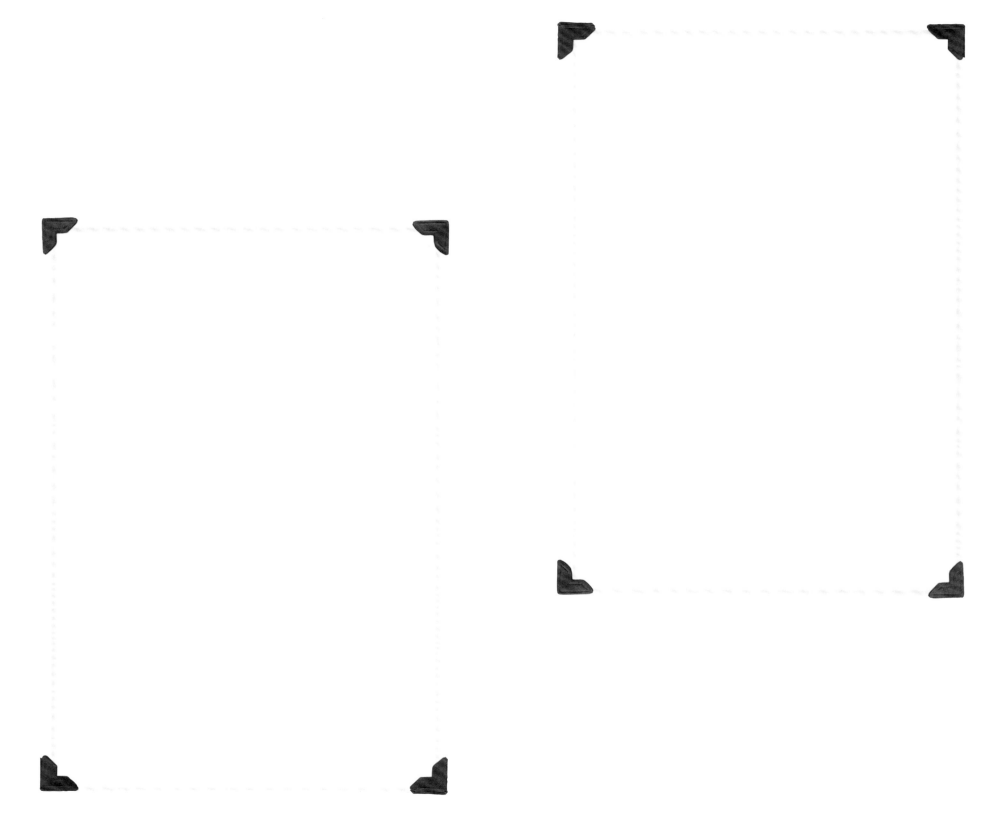

"There is no part of one's life to which one looks back in after-years with the same happy remembrance, and with the wish that one could live that part over again, as to one's college days. It seems in retrospect to have been all pleasant. Even the hardships, and the disappointments, and the seeming wrongs, and the reverses, fade out of the strong lights of the picture, and almost assume the role of the dragons which we overcame in our knightly fashion in those days of high adventure."

—President Arthur Stanley MacKenzie, 1930

# ACKNOWLEDGEMENTS
## *The Provenance of the Portrait*

This book is a testament to the adage "nobody does anything alone." It is the work, not only of many people, but also of many years.

It really began in 1970, with the appointment of the first university archivist, Charles Armour. He acquired and organized linear kilometres of archival material, and much of what appears in this book would not be available if not for his enthusiasm for historical research.

Following Charles's retirement, Michael Moosberger, Dal's second archivist, began publishing online finding aids and building digital collections. He also hired Creighton Barrett as Dal's first digital archivist. At that time, eight years ago, Mike charged Creighton with the monumental task of scanning images and records expressly in anticipation the 200th anniversary.

Creighton has been our chief point of contact with Dal's archives and we are very grateful to him and his team, the "behind the scenes" folks who have made it possible for all of us to share in the visual memories of Dalhousie: Margaret Vail, Zac Howarth-Schueler, and David Mifflen who worked the IT magic; Geoff Brown and Kathryn Harvey who did a lot of the early technical work on finding aids; and of course, the heroes here are the core archives staff who do most of the retrieval, digitization, and cataloguing. They are: Kelly Casey, Joan Chiasson, Jennifer Lambert, and Dianne Landry. We'd like to particularly mention Jennifer MacIsaac at the Agricola Archives of the Ag campus. In Halifax, Alice Albarda worked intensively on promotion of Dal history for the 200th anniversary. Shirley Vail was crucial during the final stages of bringing the manuscript together, and was patient and helpful throughout many late-night, early-morning, and through-the-weekend requests.

Despite his considerable prescience, Mike Moosberger couldn't have envisioned all the forms the 200th celebrations might take. For this commemorative book, we are all indebted to Cheryl Avery, whose idea this was in the first place. She and I are in turn indebted to Betty Jantz and Louise Barak whose 1997 *University of Saskatchewan: A Photo Album* inspired us. We also drew inspiration and images from Brian Smith's *Dalhousie University: A Time to Remember* (Harmony House, 1990) and P.B. Waite's archival research in *The Lives of Dalhousie,* volumes one and two (McGill-Queen's University Press, 1994 and 1998).

The superb project management and gifted editorial eye of Kim Pittaway and the assistance of Cheryl Avery with all things archival, even from the middle of the continent, both served this project above and beyond the call of duty. I am grateful for their generosity, collaboration, and friendship. It is without exaggeration to say that this project would not have been completed without them.

The folks who helped with the enormous task of narrowing down the "contemporary" images are: Paul Williams, Luke Smith, Fran Ornstein, Gail LeBlanc, Brenna MacNeil, Lisa Holmes, and Alison Beckett. Susan Brousseau, Martha Casey, Erin Stewart-Reid, and Chloe Westlake also helped to track down images and information. Erica

Some of the many people who had a hand in this book:

above: Design, Communications and Marketing (SP)

facing page: The Dalhousie University Archives (DA)

Gagnon was an invaluable source of both text and image, while Keri Irwin and Sheila Blair-Reid stepped in at a crucial juncture with expeditious logistical management. Jane Lombard, whose tenacity, ingenuity, sheer hard work, and brilliant detective skills served the project, deserves special mention for her return from retirement to help us navigate the institutional memory of Dalhousie.

I want to thank also the writers whose excellent words helped identify images, provided captions, and from whose interviews quotations were drawn: Dawn Morrison, Jane Affleck, Stefanie Wilson, Stephanie Rogers, Matt Reeder, Erin Stewart-Reid, Mark Campbell, Graeme Gunn, Matt Semansky, Ryan McNutt, and Evan Kelly, among others whose names I may have missed but who wrote over the years for *Alumni News*, *Dal News*, *DAL* Magazine, the *Dalhousie Gazette*, Today@Dal, the 200th anniversary website, and the 200th anniversary videos.

The wise counsel of the internal editorial board of Catherine Bagnell Styles, Sheila Blair-Reid, Kim Pittaway, and June Davidson, and the individuals across campus with whom I consulted on various stages of production all contributed to the book's current form. In particular, I am always blessed by the time I spend in conversation with our Elder-in-residence, Geri Musqua-LeBlanc.

All of this collective effort has been immeasurably improved through our partnership with Goose Lane Editions. A good editor and designer are worth their weight in gold. Paula Sarson and Julie Scriver are no exceptions. They provided much-needed perspective at the right time and thoughtful interventions in both word and image.

Finally, the greatest debt is two-fold: first to George Elliott Clarke for his wonderful poem, for agreeing, so generously and enthusiastically, to a partnership between poetry and pictures and for being our "navigator" as we move toward our next century. And thanks lastly to the photographers appearing in the credits whose art is the visual poetry to accompany the poem, especially full-time Dalhousie photographers Nick Pearce and Danny Abriel, who managed, somehow, to respond with good will and good humour to requests for custom photography in the midst of the work they do day in and day out to record Dal's memories for all of us.

# PHOTOGRAPY CREDITS & ARCHIVAL CITATIONS

We acknowledge the generous contribution of photographs and artifacts from the following individuals and institutions.

The photographers (initials in parentheses) are credited by photograph, on the page on which their work appears: Danny Abriel (DA); Fowler Bauld & Mitchell Architecture, MacLennan Jaunkalns Miller Architects (FBM/MJMA); Bruce Bottomley (BB); Natural Sciences and Engineering Research Council of Canada (NSERC); *Chronicle Herald* (CH); Richard Florizone, (RF); Patrick Fulgencio (PF); Evan Groen (EG); Mona HolmLand (MH); Arazoo Hoseyni (AH); Sidney Idemudia (SI); Wes Johnston (WJ); Mark Kays Photography (MK); Rachael Kelly (RK); Stephane Kirchhoff (SK); David MacDonald (DM); Paul McCurdy/Accomplice Content Supply Co. Halifax (PM); Ryan McNutt (RM); Findlay Muir (FM); Ocean Tracking Network (OTN); Andy Nichols (AN); Rochelle Owen (RO); Chris Parent (CP); Nick Pearce (NP); iStock Photo (iSP); Scott Pronych (SP); Debbie Rowe (DR); Robert Scheibling (RS); Skyline Studio/Accomplice Content Supply Co. (SS); Brian Smith (BS); Dalhousie University (DU).

\*

Archives and museums (credit abbreviations in parentheses) are credited by image on the page on which their holding appears. All are located in Halifax, Nova Scotia, unless otherwise noted.

Dalhousie University Archives & Museums: Nova Scotia Agricultural College (NSAC) Agricola Archives, Museum and Special Collections, Truro, Nova Scotia. (AA); Dalhousie Dentistry (DD); Dalhousie University Archives (UA); J. Gordon Duff Pharmacy Museum (PMu); Killam Library Archives, (KL); R.L. de C.H. Saunders Museum of Anatomy (MA); Thomas McCullough Museum (TM); Fountain School of Performing Arts (FSPA).

Other Archives: Halifax Municipal Archives (HA); Nova Scotia Archives (NSA); University of Saskatchewan Archives, Saskatoon, SK (US).

Archival citations for images/objects are indicated by page, clockwise from top left. Unless noted, references are to the Dalhousie University Archives. Otherwise, citations are preceded by their institution's credit abbreviations.

## 1 BUILDINGS AND BOULEVARDS

29 Edward J. Mullaly Map Collection, MS-2-46, Folder 1
30 Photograph Collection, PC1, Box 11, Folder 13, Item 1; Arthur Lismer's Dalhousie Sketches, 0000-091, Box 1, Folder 3, Item 1; (NSA) H.W. Hopkins Nova Scotia Archives Library O/S G 1129 H3 H67 1878; Memorabilia Collection, Box 1, Folder 41
31 Reference Collection, MS-1-Ref, Box 89, Folder 11
32 Reference Collection MS-1-Ref, Box 20, Folder 24
36 Lismer's Dalhousie Sketches, 0000-091, Box 1, Folder 18, Item 2
37 Photograph Collection, PC1, Box 2, Folder 7, Item 3; Reference Collection, MS-1-Ref, Box 190; (AA) NSAC Photographs UA-43, A2017-161
38 (AA) NSAC Photographs, UA-43, PB Box 1, Folder 31.1
39 Reference Collection, MS-1-Ref, Box 21, Folder 8
40 TUNS fonds, UA-10, Box 80, Folder 2, Item 1
42 (HA) City of Halifax Works Dept. photograph 102-39-1-34.1
44 Reference Collection, 2006-046, Box 1; Photograph Collection, PC1, Box 19, Folder 21, item 2; Reference Collection, MS-1-Ref, Box 180, Volume 1, Issue 5; MS-1-Ref, Box 3, Folder 31, Item 1
46 (HA) City Engineer's Office Plan Q-9-3179; Photograph Collection, PC1, Box 19, Folder 7, Item 61; PC1, Box 14, Folder 25, Item 6; Reference Collection, MS-1-Ref, Box 20, Folder 1; Memorabilia Collection, Box 3, Folder 3
47 Photograph collection, PC1 Box 42, Folder 29, Item 23

## 2 A YEAR IN THE LIFE

52 Photograph Collection, PC1, Box 8, Folder 5, Item 27; PC1, Box 14, Folder 23, Item 2; Registrar's Office fonds, UA-7
53 Registrar's Office fonds, UA-7, Box 84
54 Photograph Collection, PC1, Box 26, Folder 41; Memorabilia Collection, Box 1, Folder 38
56 Memorabilia Collection, Box 1, Folder 39; Photograph Collection, PC1, Box 13, Folder 46, Item 1
57 Memorabilia Collection, Box 1, Folder 28
62 Reference Collection, MS-1-Ref, Box 23, Box 164; MS-1-Ref, Box 25, Box 166
64 Reference Collection, MS-1-Ref, Box 172, Box 31; Photograph Collection, PC1, Box 12, Folder 48
66 Photograph Collection, PC1, Box 31, Folder 5, Item 1; PC1, Box 20, Folder 46
69 Photograph Collection, PC1, Box 9, Folder 9, Item 2; PC1, Box 9, Folder 10, Item 29
70 Memorabilia Collection, Box 1, Folder 27; (PMu) Hallway display; Memorabilia Collection, Box 1, Folder 20
71 Reference Collection MS-1-Ref, Box 21, Box 160; Photograph Collection, PC1, Box 18, Folder 23; PC1, Box 27, Folder 31

## 3 QUEST FOR KNOWLEDGE

74 Photograph Collection, PC1, Box 19, Folder 12, Item 30

76 De Mille fonds, MS-2-21, Box 1, Folder 16; McCulloch fonds, MS-2-40, SF Box 16, Folder 12; Peter B. Waite fonds, MS-2-718, PB Box 13, Folder 99

77 Memorabilia Collection, Box 1, Folder 37; Reference Collection, MS-1-Ref, Box 21, Folder 10; Thomas McCullough Museum

78 Photograph Collection, PC1, Box 27, Folder 24, Item 3

80 Photograph Collection, PC1, Box 12, Folder 47

82 Photograph Collection, PC1, Box 32, Folder 16, Item 5; PC1, Box 14, Folder 24, Item 4

83 Reference Collection, MS-1-Ref, Box 21, Folder 5; Photograph Collection, PC1, Box 31, Folder 11, Item 13; Memorabilia Collection, Box 1, Folder 17

85 Peter B. Waite fonds, MS-2-718, PB Box 13, Folder 4

86 Peter B. Waite fonds, MS-2-718, PB Box 13, Folder 56; Robert Doyle fonds, MS-3-18, Box 6, Folder 2, Item 2

87 Photograph Collection, PC1, Box 31, Folder 35, Item 16

89 Photograph Collection, PC1, Box 34, Folder 3

93 (NSA) Notman photograph, Nova Scotia Archives, acc. no. 1983-310/2573

## 4 DAL IN THE WORLD

96 B. Hinds fonds, MS-2-130, Box 8, Folder 13, Item 8

97 Photograph Collection, PC1, Box 27, Folder 29; Peter B. Waite fonds, MS-2-718, PB Box 14, Folder 4

98 Oscar Glennie Donovan fonds, MS-13-11, SF Box 57, Folder 14, Item 3; Samuel R. Balcom fonds, MS-2-128, PB Box 21, Folder 9, Item 9; Peter B. Waite fonds, MS-2-718, PB Box 14, Folder 23; Photograph Collection, PC1, Box 33, Folder 27

99 Reference Collection, MS-1-Ref, Box 161, Box 22; MS-1-Ref, Box 162, Box 22; Memorabilia Collection, 5.4 UA-23.2015-044; Reference Collection, MS-1-Ref, Box 20, Folder 12, Alumni News, April 1943

100 (AA) NSAC Photographs, UA-43, PB Box 9, Folder 32; Reference Collection, MS-1-Ref, Box 222, Folder 2, Item 2

102 Photograph Collection, PC1, Box 32, Folder 2, Item 2; PC1, Box 19, Folder 16, Item 2

104 (KL) F 1039.5 H17 C5 1971; Photograph Collection, PC1, Box 9, Folder 15, Item 1

106 Reference Collection MS-1-Ref, Box 26, Box 167; Photograph Collection, PC1, Box 32, Folder 16, Item 8

110 (US) UASC, MG411, XVII, JGD 3717; Reference Collection, MS-1-Ref, Box 21, Folder 15; Reference Collection, MS-1-Ref, Box 197

## 5 YOU WERE HERE

112 Photograph Collection, PC1, Box 2, Folder 7, Item 1

114 Lismer's Sketches, 0000-091, Box 1, Folder 4, Item 2; Photograph Collection, PC1, Box 21, Folder 16; PC1, Box 3, Folder 24, Item 2

117 Memorabilia Collection, Box 8, Folder 2

118 Photograph Collection, PC1, Box 9, Folder 6, Item 2

119 Reference Collection MS-1-Ref, Box 182; Photograph Collection, PC1, Box 9, Folder 2, Item 1; Memorabilia Collection, box 4; Photograph Collection, PC1, Box 31, Folder 30, Item 1

120 Peter B. Waite fonds, MS-2-718, PB Box 13, Folder 58; (AA) NSAC Photographs UA-43, PB Box 1, Folder 18.26

121 Photograph Collection, PC1, Box 26, Folder 17

123 Photograph Collection, PC1, Box 31, Folder 25, Item 6; Reference Collection MS-1-Ref, Box 21, Folder 6; Photograph Collection, PC1, Box 43, Folder 7, Item 6

124 Memorabilia Collection, Box 1 Folder 21; Box 2, Folder 13; Box 1, Folder 36; Reference Collection MS-1-Ref, Box 21, Folder 8; Photograph Collection, PC1, Box 24, Folder 16, Item 1; Memorabilia Collection Box 2, Folder 1

125 Photograph Collection, PC1, Box 24, Folder 10; Memorabilia Collection, Box 8, Folder 1

126 Photograph Collection, PC1, Box 11, Folder 5, Item 1

127 Memorabilia Collection, Box 2, Folder 4

128 Reference Collection, MS-1-Ref, Box 204; Photograph Collection, PC1, Box 36, Folder 23, Items 29; PC1, Box 22, Folder 4, Item 1

130 Reference Collection, MS-1-Ref, Box 21, Folder 8

131 Photograph Collection, PC1, Box 35, Folder 41, Item 1; PC1, Box 25, Folder 25, Item 1; PC1, Box 13, Folder 33, Item 1

132 Photograph Collection, PC1, Oversize Folder 23, Item 1

134 Memorabilia Collection, Box 2, Folder 11; Photograph Collection, PC1, Box 28, Folder 26; Memorabilia Collection, Box 1 Folder 32

135 Memorabilia Collection, Box 2 Folders 5 & 6; Box 1, Folder 23

Copyright © 2018 by Dalhousie University.
"The Story of Dalhousie; Or, The University as Insurgency"
copyright © 2018 by George Elliott Clarke.

All rights reserved. No part of this work may be reproduced or used in any form or by any means, electronic or mechanical, including photocopying, recording, or any retrieval system, without the prior written permission of the publisher or a licence from the Canadian Copyright Licensing Agency (Access Copyright). To contact Access Copyright, visit www.accesscopyright.ca or call 1-800-893-5777.

Edited by Paula Sarson.
Cover and page design by Julie Scriver.
Printed in Canada by Friesens.
10 9 8 7 6 5 4 3 2 1

We acknowledge the generous support of the Government of Canada, the Canada Council for the Arts, and the Government of New Brunswick.

Goose Lane Editions
500 Beaverbrook Court, Suite 330
Fredericton, New Brunswick
CANADA E3B 5X4
www.gooselane.com

Dalhousie University
Halifax, Nova Scotia,
CANADA B3H 4R2
www.dal.ca

Library and Archives Canada Cataloguing in Publication

Holmlund, Mona, author
   Dalhousie University : a 200th anniversary portrait / poetry by George Elliott Clarke ; curated by Mona Holmlund.

ISBN 978-1-77310-034-0 (hardcover)

1. Dalhousie University--History.
2. Universities and colleges--Nova Scotia--Halifax--History.
I. Clarke, George Elliott, 1960-, writer of added text  II. Title.

LE3.D32H65 2018      378.716'225      C2018-901157-2